Life Changers

Seventeen Kingdom Principles
Every Believer Should Know

WILLIE A. CRANE

LIFE CHANGERS
Seventeen Kingdom Principles Every Believer Should Know

iUniverse books may be ordered through booksellers or by contacting:

iUniverse
1663 Liberty Drive
Bloomington, IN 47403
www.iuniverse.com
1-800-Authors (1-800-288-4677)

Because of the dynamic nature of the Internet, any web addresses or links contained in this book may have changed since publication and may no longer be valid. The views expressed in this work are solely those of the author and do not necessarily reflect the views of the publisher, and the publisher hereby disclaims any responsibility for them.

Any people depicted in stock imagery provided by Thinkstock are models, and such images are being used for illustrative purposes only. Certain stock imagery © Thinkstock.

ISBN: 978-1-4917-7062-7 (sc)
ISBN: 978-1-4917-7063-4 (hc)
ISBN: 978-1-4917-7064-1 (e)

Library of Congress Control Number: 2015909785

Print information available on the last page.

iUniverse rev. date: 06/27/2015

All scripture references are from *The King James Study Bible (previously published as The Liberty Annotated Study Bible and as The Annotated Study Bible, King James Version) Copyright 1988 by Liberty University*

CONTENTS

ACKNOWLEDGEMENTS

Thank you to:

Bishop Leroy Davis and First Lady Helen Davis
And the Word of Faith Christian Center Church Family

This book is dedicated to

The late Earlene Crane- Miles for being the greatest mother a son could ever ask for.

To my daughter Nia, I thank God everyday for the gift that is you. My prayer is that you will always live your life by the principles of the Word of God and fulfill the awesome calling that is on your life. You are my Joy!

To Kimberly Pfeifer, Your love, support, and encouragement have allowed me to finish this book. It is my prayer that I add as much value to your life as you have added to mine. With all my love!

To God the Father, Jesus the Son and the Holy Spirit, for without you I can do nothing.

INTRODUCTION

The truest measure of your Christian faith is to know, to understand, and display the heart of Jesus. The greatest desire of God the Father and the Holy Spirit is that we come to know Jesus Christ as the savior of the world. The greatest desire of Jesus is that we receive Him to gain access to the Father and His Kingdom. I have come to know that God wants every believer to understand the Kingdom of God and how it operates, thus the reason for this book. In it I will share with you the Kingdom of God and the principles that govern the kingdom you are now apart of. Just like in the natural world, if you were suddenly place in a foreign land as a new citizen you would have to learn about the laws that govern that land. It would be nearly impossible to have success in that land without the ability to communicate effectively. It would also be difficult to make progress without knowing and understand the laws that protect you and the rights you are afforded by being a citizen of the land. All of these things are important to know so that you can operate and fulfill the purposes you were sent there to accomplish.

I have often said, "You will either live your life by the principles of the Word or by the practices of the world." The principles represent how the Kingdom of God operates which is totally different than the practices of the world. Any success that is attained, maintained and sustained is done by practicing kingdom principles. God has established His kingdom principles throughout the bible to help us govern this earthly kingdom in the same manner in which He governs His heavenly kingdom. He has given His son's blood as the necessary payment to atone for our sins and as our earthly example of how to conduct ourselves inside this kingdom. He has also given us His Holy Spirit to lead us into a right understanding of what can and can't be done in the kingdom of God.

After reading, studying and understanding the principles that are written and explained in this book you will be able to access Gods best and to operate as true kings and priests in the earth and as inheritors of the Kingdom of God.

Life Changers

Kingdom Principles Every Believer Should Know

"You will either live your life by the principles of the Word or by the practices of the world."

Willie A. Crane

CHAPTER 1

The Kingdom Principle of Faith

"But without faith it is impossible to please him: for he that cometh to God must believe that he is, and that he is a rewarder of them that diligently seek him." Hebrews 11:6

It couldn't have been a more perfect summer day. The sun was shining the sky was blue and covered with those cotton looking clouds that allowed you to call out images of different animals in the sky. As a nine year old I have to admit that was one of my favorite pass times. I had always been curious about those kinds of wonders. Curious about who made them and how. I didn't know that this was going to be the day that would change my life forever. As I was standing there gazing up at the sky and wondering about all the beauty I was beholding I was interrupted by a friend's question. I didn't notice him standing there before but there he was right next to me looking up just as I was. When I looked over at him he met my puzzled look with one of his own and asked, "Do you believe in God?" As I pondered the question and searched my thoughts for an answer I simply said, "Naw."

He said, "why not." I said, "Because you can't see him." Being satisfied with my response he quickly ran off to play some more. Just then I heard a voice that was clear and soft. He asked me a question also. I didn't know if the voice was coming from inside me or externally. All I know is that it was crystal clear. He asked me, "Can you see the wind blow?" At that very moment what had been a calm breezeless day suddenly changed and a cool breeze swept across my face. Standing there in amazement and complete assurance that God himself was speaking he said these words to me. "The things that you cannot see made the thing that you can, so which is more real?" I was convinced that God was real and I had to get to know him better. I didn't realize that I had begun a journey with God. The beginning, just as Hebrews 11:6 states is to believe that he is. Hebrews 11:6 marks the first declaration of our faith as believers. Without this declaration it is impossible to please him.

Matthew 6:33 says: "But seek ye first the kingdom of God, and his righteousness and all these things shall be added unto you." I came to understand this scripture and its significance to my life when I was very young. It is one of the foundational cornerstones to understanding God, purpose, your assignment in life and faith. To understand this scripture and its correct meaning we have to dissect some of the words used. Jesus instructs us to seek for the kingdom of God and its righteousness. What does he really mean? Are we to look for it on a map? Can it be found geographically? The kingdom of God and its righteousness must be something that can be found or else he wouldn't have instructed us to seek to find it. The Kingdom of God represents the order of God, the principles of God, the laws of God and the precepts of God. Its righteousness represents its right understanding. Simply put it is the understanding of the way God governs his kingdom. A King is one of supreme authority, rulership and power. I often wondered why God would give the children of Isreal land that was occupied by someone else. The scripture says that the Earth is the Lords and the fullness there of. Jesus being the supreme King and Lord of all the earth and all that it possesses and inhabits has the authority to give to anyone whatever he pleases because everything and everyone belongs to him.

The Lord's Prayer is the perfect example of God's intention. In the Lord's Prayer we are taught to say, "Our Father which art in heaven, Hallowed be thy name. Thy kingdom come. Thy will be done in earth, as it is in heaven." Jesus taught his disciples to pray that God's kingdom come. In other words he told them to pray that the same laws, precepts and principles that govern heaven be used to govern the earth also. Thy will be done indicates that it is indeed God's will that the earth realm be governed the same way heaven is being governed. The only difference is that Jesus the King of Kings gave back to mankind (kings and priests) the authorities to govern, rule, and manage the earth the same way he governs heaven. With the guidance of the Holy Spirit this is indeed possible and is the supreme will of God for us as inhabitants of this earthly kingdom.

During my prayer time I asked the Holy Spirit to reveal to me the principle of faith. As He spoke to me He gave me a definition that has clarified the principle of faith for me. He instructed me that from that point on I was to teach the principle his way. He said, "Faith is hearing the Word of God, understanding the Word of

God, believing the Word of God and applying the Word of God." The important part to remember is that all of the promises of God are received by faith. It is the way the believer receives from God who is in the spiritual realm and causes it to manifest in the natural realm. Whenever one of the pillars of faith is missing there will be no manifestation. All four of the pillars must be in place in order for the principle to deliver what has been requested. It is impossible to have faith in something you have never heard of. That is what the scripture means in Romans 10:14 which says, "… how shall they believe on him whom they have not heard? And how shall they hear with out a preacher?" Hearing the word of God is the first pillar of the Kingdom principle of faith.

As Jesus explained the parable of the sower in the book of St. Matthew chapter 13 verses 19, He started by saying, "When any one hears the word of the kingdom, and understands it not, then comes the wicked one, and catches away that which was sown in his heart. This is he who received seed by the way side." Notice it is only when the word is not understood that the enemy can steal it out of the person's heart. All through out scripture the word of God instructs us to get a complete understanding. Understanding the word of God is the second pillar of the Kingdom principle of faith.

Once you have heard the word of God and you understand it then the third pillar of faith can be realized, that is to believe the word. The reason we can believe the word of God is because it is truth. Not that it possesses truth but that it is truth. Jesus said, "Sanctify them through thy truth, thy word is truth." St. John 17:17 the only truth that exists is the word of God. The strength of my belief should always be rooted and grounded in the truth.

The fourth pillar that needs to be established is the pillar of applying the word of God. In the book of James chapter 1 verses 22, 25 he instructs us that we are to be doers of the word and not hearers only because only the doers of the word are blessed in what he does.

Faith in its purest definition is the hearing, understanding, belief and application of God's kingdom principles. Faith is not just believing but acting on what you believe. James 2:17-18 says, "Even so faith, if it hath not works, is dead, being alone. Yea, a man may say, Thou hast faith, and I have works: show me thy faith without thy works, and I will show thee my faith by my works."

Let's take a few scriptures about faith and substitute this definition in place of the word faith. Remember faith is the hearing understanding, belief and application of the Word of God.

1. Hebrews 11:6 says, "But without faith (the hearing, understanding, belief and application of God's kingdom principles) it is impossible to please him."
2. Hebrews 6:12 says, "That they be not slothful, but followers of them who through faith (the hearing, understanding, belief and application of God's kingdom principles) and patience inherit the promises."
3. II Corinthians 5:7 says, "For we walk by faith (the hearing, understanding, belief and application and of God's kingdom principles) not by sight."

4. 1 John 5:4 says, "For whatsoever is born of God overcometh the world: and this is the victory that overcometh the world even our faith." (the hearing, understanding, belief and application of God's kingdom principles)

Once again, faith in its purest definition is the hearing, understanding, belief and application of God's kingdom principles.

What is a Principle?

Let's take a moment and define what a principle is. The definition of principle is the ultimate source, origin or cause of something. It also means a fundamental truth, law, doctrine, or motivating force. It can also mean a rule of conduct especially the right conduct. When studying the principles in the Word of God I came across this scripture: Romans 1:20 it says, "For the invisible things of him from the creation of the world are clearly seen, being understood by the thing that are made, even his eternal power and Godhead; so that they are without excuse." What the scripture means is that we can come to understand spiritual things (the invisible things of him from the creation of the world are clearly seen) by observing how natural thing work (being understood by the things that are made). When we look at the natural principles we can come to understand how spiritual principles work. Each principle has its own application and thus has its own outcome. Although each principle has its own application and outcome all principles have the same four characteristics.

To understand principles we must first come to understand its characteristics. All principles share these four common characteristics:

1. All principles work 100% of the time. It has been said that science cannot call an experiment a principle until it yields the same results 100 times after 100 experiments. This indicates that the principle is indeed perfect. If at anytime the experiment yields a different result it cannot be classified as a principle.
2. All principles are impersonal. They have no respect of person. A principle simply does what a principle does.
3. A principle can be violated but never broken.
4. Once you understand the principle you can predict its outcome.

Earlier we said that Romans 1:20 stated that we can understand spiritual thing by observing how natural thing function. For example let's take the natural law of gravity and apply the four characteristics of a principle and see if this is true. First we said that a principle works 100% of the time. Using the principle of gravity, which states that an object will fall at the rate of 32 ft. per second when released we can see that gravity when tested will yield the same results every time it is tested. Basically, it says that what goes up must come down. If I toss a pencil in the air 100 times it will come down 100 times. This indicates that the law is perfect. Secondly we said that a principle is impersonal. It has no respect of person. It will simply do what it does. Let's say that I was holding a new born baby in my hands and accidentally lost control of the baby, gravity cannot say "oh no that's a baby" and not take its toll on the child. It has no respect of person it simply does what it does. We also said that the third characteristic of a principle is that a principle can be violated but never broken. We can see this application when observing an airplane take off and land. When an airplane takes off it has to violate the law of gravity. Remember the law has been violated but not broken thus proving the third characteristic. We know this because when the airplane has to land it is the law of gravity that brings it down. If the law of gravity had been broken it would have ceased to exist thus preventing the airplane from ever coming down. The fourth characteristic is also in operation when the plane takes off and lands. The fourth characteristic states that once you understand the principle you can predict its outcome. We are able to predict the airplanes landing because we now understand how the law of gravity works.

Spiritual principles as well as natural principles all share the same four characteristics. All spiritual principles work 100% of the time and yield the same results every time when they are applied. Spiritual principles have no respect of person. They will work for whoever will work them. Spiritual principles can be violated but never broken and the outcome of spiritual principles can be predicted once they are understood.

Faith your Master Key

My mentor would often remind me that God will pass over a million people who have a need to get to one person who has faith. Contrary to popular belief God is not attracted to your needs, emotional crying or pleading through attempted prayer. He is only attracted to faith. I worked in a school building once where the head custodian had a master key. This key could open all the doors and give him access to all the rooms in the school. Even though the other custodians were given specific keys that opened the individual doors of the building the head custodian was given the master key that could open all the doors. In the book of Matthew chapter 16 verses 19 Jesus said to Peter and the other disciples "and I will give unto thee the keys of the kingdom of heaven." Keys represent authority. This meant that Peter and the others would have the right to access and enter the kingdom for themselves. Anytime you are given keys you have been given the authority to access what the keys will open. Faith is the master key that will access all that God has. Faith also gives you the authority to operate like God. What pleases God most; is that we act like and live like we understand his kingdom and the authority he has given us. This means living by faith, the hearing, understanding, belief and application of his kingdom principles. God has given to each person who accepts His son Jesus as their Lord and Savior the power of the Holy Spirit to access His heavenly kingdom right here on Earth. Living by faith, the hearing, understanding, belief and application of God's principles will cause God to be pleased with your life.

After you have heard the message of salvation and receive by faith the Lord Jesus Christ the greatest and most important message that you must consistently hear is the message of faith. I have learned that Satan doesn't care if the believer goes to church. He only cares that you never learn about faith. Many have gotten away from preaching about the kingdom of God and faith and have resorted to emotional hype as a substitute for a true move of God. It has always been and will always be God's will that His children live by faith. Hebrews 1:17 and Habakkuk 2:4 states that, "The just shall live by faith." To live any other way as a believer is to live in rebellion to God's word. Faith causes you to pursue purpose, labors with power, give uncommon praise and lives by the principle of meaningful prayer.

Faith = Victory

1 John 5:4 says, "Whatsoever is born of God overcometh the world: and this is the victory that overcometh the world even our faith."

In this passage John tells us that the hearing, understanding, belief and application of God's principles are what cause us to be victorious in every situation we may face from the world. The world represents the order of Satan or the systematic ways contrary to God's laws and principles. Faith has the ability to super exceed anything the enemy can bring. This is the reason why it is imperative that the believer learn and master the kingdom principle of faith. Paul instructed us in Ephesians 6:11 to put on the whole or entire armor of God so that we may be able to stand against the wiles of the devil. In verse 16 of Ephesians chapter 6 he states, "Above all, taking the shield of faith, wherewith ye shall be able to quench all the fiery darts of the wicked. **Above all** indicates this is the most important piece of your battle armor. It is through faith that you will have the ability to withstand **all** of the attacks of the wicked one.

The Faith Process

"For every principle, for every prophecy and for every promise there is a faith process to bring it to pass."

Bishop I.V. Hilliard

In **Mark 4:26-29** Jesus explains the faith process by using the parable of the seed. He says, "So is the kingdom of God, as if a man should cast seed into the ground; and should sleep, and rise night and day, and the seed should spring and grow up, he knoweth not how. For the earth bringeth forth fruit of herself; first the blade, then the ear, after that the full corn in the ear, but when the fruit is brought forth immediately he putteth in the sickle, because the harvest is come." The faith process begins with the words you speak. This is the seed Jesus spoke of in the parable. Faith is always initiated by our words. Second, the faith seed must be planted. The scripture says that the earth bringeth forth fruit of herself. The earth represents the heart of man. Not someone else's heart but yours. It is the condition of your heart that helps determines the harvest time. My office is located directly in front of 20 to 25 acres of farm land. Every year the owner of the property plants either corn or beans. One year as he was preparing the field the Lord spoke to me as I was watching. He softly spoke and said," The first law of the harvest is not the seed must be planted (as I had often heard) but the ground must be tilled." As the Lord spoke the Holy Spirit quickly brought back to my remembrance the parable of the sower. In each case the sower distributed seeds but only the ground that had been broken up was prepared to receive the seed. The word of God says that only that heart brought forth a tremendous harvest. One other critical aspect of the faith process is patience. Patience is the ability to remain constant when everything around you comes against what you believe. Verse 27 says: "and should sleep and raise night and day, and the seed should spring and grow up, he knoweth not how." This verse indicates that there will be a time when there will be no indication in the natural realm that the promise will come to pass. This is where your patience is most critical. When a farmer plants seed into the ground he doesn't return the next day to see if the earth is processing the seed. He simply trusts that the earth is doing what it does even though he may not fully understand the details of what the earth does and how it is done. Verse 28 says: "first the blade, then the ear, after that the full corn in the ear." When you start to see an indication of the promise coming to pass it will begin as a blade and not the full manifestation. Again patience is required because the time of harvest has not fully come. We as believers have to be very careful in understanding this principle because it is possible to think that the blade is all of the blessing. If we do this and attempt to access the harvest we will be disappointed because we didn't allow the blessing to mature so that it can bless us and be a blessing to others. When a farmer first sees the blade he is excited with anticipation that a harvest is closer today than it was yesterday. He knows that he has to continue to protect the blade by removing anything from the soil that may hinder the seed so that it can mature into a full ear of corn. Even so with us we must continue to search our hearts to remove any bitterness or unforgivness that can cause the seeds growth to be hindered. Once, this is done you can expect to see the ear and then the full corn in the ear.

The Five Expectations of Faith

> Hebrews 11: 1 says, "Now faith is the substance of things hoped for, the evidence of things not seen.

When the believer is operating in faith he has an earnest expectation that what he believes for has already come to pass. He is simply expecting the manifestation of what he has faith for. When you are in faith there are five key things to expect before you see the manifestation. Those five expectations are as follows:

A Specific Plan of Action

First I'm expecting God to give me a **specific plan of action.** As you look at the believers in the bible whenever they asked God for something he would give them a specific plan of action. In the book of Joshua chapter 6 verses 3 thru 4 God gives Joshua a specific plan of action. God tells Joshua in verse 3 and 4 "and ye shall compass the city, all ye men of war, and go round about the city once. Thus shall thou do six days. And seven priests shall bear before the ark seven trumpets of rams' horns: and the seventh day ye shall compass the city seven times, and the priests shall blow with the trumpets." Here God gives him a specific plan of action for the battle. In the latter verses God also explains to him what will happen when he follows his specific instructions. Joshua and the children of Isreal followed God's specific plan of action and were successful in capturing the city of Jericho for the Lord.

Often times as believer we miss out on God's best for our lives because we fail to realize that God works by his own principles. He cannot and will not break those principles for anyone. When you pray and are in faith expect God to give you first his specific plan of action. Following this plan with complete obedience will bring you what you have requested.

The Wisdom of God

Second, expect **the wisdom of God**. My definition of wisdom is the ability to choose the correct kingdom principle for your situation. James 1:5 says, "If any of you lack wisdom, let him ask of God, that gives to all men liberally and upbraideth not; and it shall be given him." God says, "If you want to know what principle to use to vindicate yourself from your situation, just ask me and I will give it to you." Not to long ago I was in a restaurant with a friend and witnessed a waitress encounter a very unhappy customer. As the customer started to raise their voice and draw attention to the situation the waitress reacted with an equally loud and aggressive response. Within seconds an argument ensued. When the manager was informed he calmly came over and listened to the customer concern. After evaluating the situation he offered a solution that satisfied the customer. At that very moment I thought about Proverbs 15:1. It says, "A soft answer turns away wrath; but grievous words stir up anger." The manager applied the wisdom of God to the situation and received the outcome he had expected.

The Supernatural Favor of God

When I am in faith the third expectation is for the **supernatural favor of God.** My definition of the favor of God is God causing other people to use their gifts, talents, time and treasure to help you. Whenever God calls you to an assignment he calls others also to help you. Early one morning I left for work as usual and forgot to bring money for lunch. I was concerned that I would be stuck so far away from home without any cash. As I started to pray and ask God for direction on what I should do the Holy Spirit spoke to me and said, "I have taken care of it." As the day progressed and lunchtime was approaching I decided to help God out. I approached a colleague and asked if he wanted to go to lunch. He said, "Yes." I said to him, "you're going to have to pay this time." He said, "That's fine." At that very moment I sensed the displeasure of the Holy Spirit. I knew I hade manipulated the situation and the Holy Spirit was letting me know what he thought of my help. He calmly and sternly said "I have taken care of it." When we got to the restaurant my friend asked me about my birthday that had just passed a few days ago. As I was talking the cashier over heard the conversation and said "since it was your birthday I'm going to by your lunch today." The Holy Spirit without hesitation said, "As I said I took care of it." Needless to say I was humbled and excited at the same time. I had just experienced the **favor of God**. Those kinds of situations happen quite often. I now understand that it is a part of my inheritance to expect Gods' supernatural favor.

A miracle of God

The fourth expectation is for a **miracle of God.** A miracle of God occurs when he intervenes supernaturally in our situation. Whenever Satan attempts to derail the plan of God and goes outside the boundaries of his jurisdiction we have the right to expect a supernatural move of God to bring about his desired purpose. To receive a miracle from God also requires an act of obedience on the part of the recipient. In Genesis chapter

14 Moses and the children of Isreal found themselves in a very difficult position. The approaching Egyptians were coming up behind them and mountains were on each side of them and the sea in front of them. God instructs Moses to tell the people to go forward. At that very moment God gives Moses a plan of action. He tells him to stretch out his hand with the staff over the sea. When Moses obeyed God the sea opened up and the children of Isreal walked over to the other side on dry ground. The expectation of a miracle of God is an essential part of the believer's faith. We are assured in the book of Isaiah chapter 59 verse 19b that "when the enemy shall come in like a flood the Spirit of the Lord shall lift up a standard against him." God is always prepared to intervene on our behalf with a miracle when the need arises.

The Strength to Endure

The fifth expectation is the **strength to endure until the manifestation happens.** In any fight it is expected that the combatants will at some point become wearied and tired. The mental stress and physical fatigue will indeed set in. Just like a physical fight a spiritual fight can and will require you to expend energy. As a rule of thumb we are all products of how we have been trained. Over the years I have come to know that there are many things that are said in church circles that sound scriptural but are not scripturally sound. One such church cliché states that trials come to make you strong. Let's examine the logic behind that statement. If trials come to make you strong we should all be Herculean in strength spiritually. In every fight I have ever witnessed where one of the combatants was taking punishment he did not appear to be getting stronger from every blow he was receiving. It was however just the opposite. With every blow he was being weakened. This is also true with us as believers. When we take to many spiritual blows our faith is weakened. How then do I sustain my spiritual strength when the enemy is attacking? The scripture says that the joy of the Lord is our strength. Psalms 16:11 states, "in thy presence is the fullness of joy." It is in God's presence that we find our strength. In essence it is our continued communion with God through prayer that keeps us strong. Trials were never meant to make us strong they were only created to develop our patience. James 1:3 states, "Knowing this, that the trying of your faith works patience." If you are facing a trial or test rest assured that God knows that you are already equipped with everything you need to get through it. Remember patience is the ability to remain constant through it all.

Chapter 1

The Kingdom Principle of Faith

Overview

The Kingdom of God

(4) Characteristics of a Principle

- All principles work 100% of the time
- All principles are impersonal
- A principle can be violated but never broken
- Once you understand a principle you can predict its outcome.

Faith is your Master Key

Faith =Victory

The Faith Process

The (5) Expectations of Faith

1. Plan of Action
2. The Wisdom of God
3. The Favor of God
4. A Miracle from God
5. The Strength to Endure

CHAPTER 2

The Kingdom Principle of Love

"For God so loved the world that he gave his only begotten Son, that whosoever believeth in him should not perish, but have everlasting life."
St. John 3:16

Standing outside of the hospital room awaiting the birth of my first child, I was overcome by a gamut of emotions. My thoughts were all over the spectrum. Concerned that I would not be a good father I began to cry. As I positioned myself in the opposite direction to avoid anyone who may have walked by, I began to pray. "Lord you said in your word that I can cast all of my cares upon you because you care for me. This life you have placed in my care is the greatest responsibility I have ever faced and I know I cannot do this without you. I surrender this child's life back to you now. Teach me to be the kind of father you would want me to be for her." As I finished that prayer I felt the peace of God inside me. I knew that raising this child would be the challenge of my life but I was sure that God would guide me. When Nia was born and placed in the maternity room I stood there outside the room staring at her through the glass. I didn't notice my mother when she walked up behind me. She placed her hand gently on my shoulder and said "I bet you had no idea that kind of love even existed." She was right I had no idea. I knew beyond a shadow of a doubt that I loved this little girl with everything in me. My mother hugged me and said congratulations. With one of those smiles that spoke of great understanding she kissed me and said good night. When I was allowed to go inside and hold her for the first time that wonderful feeling of love seemed to intensify. Just then that small still calm voice of God said "just as you love her with your whole being it is with my whole being that I love you." From that moment I had a clear understanding of the scripture that states that God is love. The Holy Spirit reminded me that God does not possess love but instead is love. The very essence of God is love.

Love is not a feeling but it is your intrinsic desire and commitment to meet another persons needs unconditionally.

One of the reasons God created mankind in his image and in his likeness is to have someone who was capable and willing to reciprocate the love he gives to us. In every aspect of God's being he exhibits his love. Even when God chastens us the word of God says that he does this because he is unconditionally committed to our well being.

The (4) Pillars of Love

Galatians 5:22-23 tells us of the many attributes of God. The scripture says, "But the fruit of the Spirit is love, joy, peace, long-suffering, gentleness, goodness, faith, meekness and temperance."

All of these are an attribute of God's perfect love. Think of it this way. Jesus the holy one of God represents a strong tree that has many branches. St John 15:1 indicates that we are the branches and it is the branches that produce the fruit. It is when Christ lives through us that we are able to demonstrate his love.

From this point on I will discuss each one of the foundational truths in groups of four. I call this the "Principle of the Power of Four."

Each principle has (4) quadrants. Think of each principle as a table. The legs of the table or pillars represent quadrants. The table as long as it is supported by all 4 pillars can stand firm even when there is added pressure applied to the top of it.

The difficulty comes when we try to support items on the top of the table with one or more of the legs missing.

It is possible for the table to stand with only 3 legs. However, the added weight on top must be strategically placed in order for the table to remain standing. In essence this means added pressure or weight on the other three legs.

It is however not possible for the table to stand when 2 of the legs are missing thus rendering the table totally ineffective for its intended use.

Love through the truth of His Word

The 4 pillars of love are **truth, security, sacrifice** and **obedience**. Let's look at each one individually. **First is truth**. It is impossible to love someone or enter into a loving relationship without truth being one of the foundational pillars that helps support the relationship. Truth also produces the attribute of trustworthiness. How much a person values truth, the essence of the word of God, will determine how much they can be trusted. If a person cannot be trusted it is impossible for true love to grow. If love is the unconditional commitment to another's well being then truth has to be an absolute way of life and not just something we consider for our sake.

Security through His Presence

The second pillar of love is security. Love provides the ultimate level of security. Paul asks the question and makes this definitive statement in the book of Romans 8:35, 38-39. Who shall separate us from the love of Christ? Shall tribulation, or distress, or persecution, or famine, or nakedness, or peril, or sword? For I am persuaded, that neither death, nor life, nor angels, nor principalities, nor powers, nor things present, nor things to come, nor height, nor depth, nor any other creature, shall be able to separate us from the love of God, which is in Christ Jesus our Lord. The scripture is very clear that nothing shall be able to separate God's love from us however the question remains is there anything that can separate your love from God? What an incredible declaration of security through love.

Sacrifice through His Work

The third pillar is sacrifice. Sacrifice is your willingness to go above and beyond your initial expectation for the betterment of someone else. Sacrifice also implies giving. The word of God says that God so loved the world that he gave his only begotten son. Here God expresses his love in a way that defines who he is. There will never be another sacrifice that equals God's sacrificial offering of his own son for us. One of the true measurements of love is through sacrifice. What have you sacrificed for God and what have you sacrificed for others to help enhance the relationship you share?

Obedience as a way of Life

The fourth pillar is obedience. Jesus in demonstrating his love for God was obedient to the will of God even unto the cross. How can one endure such torment, disrespect, shame and rejection? Hebrews chapter 12 verse 2 says, "Looking unto Jesus the author and finisher of our faith; who for the joy that was set before him endured the cross, despising the shame, and is set down on the right hand of the throne of God." I believe the joy that he set before him was the continued thought of pleasing the Father and being reunited with the Father again along with the end result of seeing God's children redeemed and set free from the bondage of sin. Obedience is the act of carrying out commands. Obedience differs from compliance, which is behavior influenced by peers, and from conformity, which is behavior intended to match that of the majority. In St. John 14:15 Jesus says, "If you love me, keep my commandments. Here Jesus commands us to demonstrate love for him through our obedience in keeping his commandments. Obedience to God is the strongest and most important pillar of the four. When there is no obedience to the will of God we forfeit the benefits that God has for us. Without obedience there can be no sense of security and no peace. When all four attributes are present we can expect and enjoy a fruitful loving relationship. I believe there is no greater need than love both to give it and to receive it. Love is the reason mankind was created to both give and receive Godly love and it is the reason mankind was redeemed.

As a father I have learned that the greatest thing I can do for my daughter rested in the 4 expressions of love. I knew that I would be the representation of what love looks like in her eyes. I also knew that I had to demonstrate the expressions of love by living out truth, security, sacrifice and obedience before her. Truth is simply the essence of Gods word. Jesus said, "My words are truth." Security is the sense of knowing that when needs rise those who are capable of meeting those needs will do so even if it means going above and beyond their initial expectations. It is every father's responsibility to help develop and bring his children's spirit forward in the principle of love. Years ago when I was a younger man there was a billboard close to the church I attended. It always caught my attention because of what it said. I remember being offended and curious at the same time. Offended because I thought it was an attack on our culture only and curious because I wondered how many would take it to heart. The billboard had a young child no more than five years old leaning on a table with his chin on his folded hands and a sad look on his face. The words next to his face were, Santa Claus, the Easter Bunny, the Tooth fairy and daddy. Children soon stop believing in those they never see. That bill board made a definite impact on me. I vowed that when I had children they would come to know me by the demonstration of my love through my presence.

It is through the relationship with the father that the children learn the principles of love. When my daughter was born I was the first to hold her. There was such an overwhelming commitment in my heart for her that I knew I would be willing to sacrifice everything necessary for her greater good. Love expresses itself through feelings and emotions but love itself is not a feeling or an emotion it is however a commitment to another's well being.

It is and always has been the responsibility of the father to help develop and mature his children spiritually. Through the four pillars of love we can see the positive effects the father's presence can have on the child's development. When the father is rooted and grounded in the truth of the word of God he is properly equipped to provide the correct spiritual guidance the child needs. The four pillars (truth, security, sacrifice and obedience) are of course spiritual and manifest themselves naturally. Let's take a look at each one of the four pillars individually as they pertain to the purposes of the father and how they work.

When a father is rooted and grounded he lives his life by the first pillar of love which is the truth of the word of God. He demonstrates the Godly behavior that is outlined in the book of 1 Corinthians chapter 13 verses 4 thru 7. The word of God says, "Love suffers long, and is kind; love does not envy; love does not brag on itself, is not puffed up. Doth not behave itself unseemly, seeks not her own, is not easily provoked, keeps no account of evil. Rejoices not in iniquity, but rejoices in the truth. Bears all things, believeth all things, and hopes for all things endure all things." The father teaches through the demonstration of Godly love toward all people and in doing so he reinforces the kind of behavior that is required and expected of us by God's.

When a father is rooted and grounded and lives his life by the truth of Gods word he establishes for his family and all who comes in contact with him the second pillar of love which is a sense of security through his presence. The family should feel safe and protected when the father is around. When love is not demonstrated by the father the children grow up never understanding the emotional peace that is transmitted from the father because of his presence. The pillar of security is vital in the support of healthy relationships. It should begin with our natural fathers and end with our spiritual Father.

As a young boy growing up in the neighborhood there were very few fathers around. I specifically remember the Thomas family because they were the only family unit in our projects that had both mother and father present and living under the bonds of marriage. That concept alone was a foreign one for me and all of the other kids in the neighborhood. I was always puzzled why the children spoke of their father with such fear. Not the reverence type of fear but the kind that makes you afraid for your well being. When they spoke about their father Mr. Thomas it was always with an uneasiness that frightened me. It was even worse when he would come out to the playground to get them to come inside for the evening. I always felt like they were not safe in their own home. They dreaded messing up for fear of their father. Even though I had no concept of what a father was supposed to be I knew that if that was it I wanted no parts of one. We often have the same distorted view of God. We believe he is some cosmic being sitting on the edge of the universe waiting for us to mess up so he can punish us with an everlasting punishment. Since many of us had no real reference of what a loving caring father was we had and still have a hard time believing that God is just that a loving and caring father.

When a father is rooted and grounded and lives his life by the truth of God's word and provides a sense of security through his presence he is able to erect the third pillar which is the pillar of sacrifice through his work. Many have come to believe that work means to have when in essence the word work in its original meaning means to become. God told Adam in the book of Genesis to become the master of the Earth to have dominion over it and to cultivate it and manage its resources. Work also refers to purpose. What you become is in direct correlation to your purpose in life. It is what you were intended to do and become. Going above and beyond your initial expectations to meet the needs of others is our ultimate sacrifice. When we become what we were supposed to be all who come in contact with us are blessed because of what we have become. This is God's original intent for us to express his glory through our work. The scripture says that we are to let our light so shine before men that they may see your good works (what we have become according to purpose) and glorify your Father which is in heaven.

When a father is rooted and grounded and lives his life by the truth of God's word. He demonstrates his love through sacrifice, security through his work and obedience in everything he does. He is trustworthy because he is obedient to the word and all that God commands. Obedience to the word of God is the ultimate demonstration of your love to God. Jesus said, "If you love me keep my commandments." (St. John 14:15)

Having a heavenly Father who loves you unconditionally is the greatest thing we could have ever asked for. His love goes beyond our understanding. Take a moment and think about the love God has for you and your love for him. It is through his commitment to you and your obedience to him that your relationship is made strong, healthy and secure.

Chapter 2

The Kingdom Principle of Love

Chapter Overview

The Four Pillars of Love

1. Love through the truth of God's word.
2. Security through his presence.
3. Sacrifice through his work. (purpose)
4. Obedience as a way of life.

CHAPTER 3

The Kingdom Principle of Purpose

"To everything there is a season, and a time to every purpose under the heaven." Ecclesiastes 3:1

I was at a wonderful show just recently and one of the featured singers was a young man who had just previously won a singing contest and was there to perform his song. I had never seen him before nor been introduced to him. The mister of ceremony introduced him and spoke these words concerning him. He said, "Here is a young man who is truly an old soul." I knew exactly what he meant when the young man approached the stage and began to sing. His voice was polished and smooth and he had an air about him that spoke of a great maturity. His song connected with the older patrons in the audience and left me wondering how such an old soul inhabited this young man's body. He dressed very conservatively unlike the teens of today and he spoke softly and confidently. That young man made me think of a statement my older sister of two years made once. My mother asked her why she liked listening to the songs of the sixties and seventies as opposed to the music that was popular at that time. Her reply was,

"I guess I was just born at the wrong time." I later found out that my sister often thought about and pondered on the very questions that all of us will have to answer at some point in our lives. She had begun to ask herself, what was the meaning of her existence? Without having been exposed to the correct information to satisfy her question she concluded on her own that she must have been born at the wrong time.

Like my sister all of mankind will come to a point where they will question their existence. Often we will go through life seeking to find an answer to the questions that plague us and never turn to the true source that can answer all of those questions. I have come to understand that every person will be faced with finding the answers to these five questions in life. First is the question that states, who am I? Second is the question, why am I here? The third question is where am I from? The fourth question is what can I do? The fifth question is where am I going? Each one of those questions has to be answered in order to enjoy the quality of life God intended for us all.

My definition of purpose is this. It is the original intent or the reason for something's existence. Only the creator of a thing can determine why it exists and what it is supposed to accomplish. To seek answers to those five questions outside of the creator is only guessing at best. It is impossible for another product to tell another product why it is here and what it is supposed to accomplish. The answer to those questions can only be found in one place and that is the mind of the creator of the thing. I have a good friend named Don Higgins who wrote a computer program that I use for my business. When Don was explaining the program he did it with such excitement and enthusiasm it made me want to know more about what it could do. Don explained and explained and explained what this program could do. When he finished going over the program I was sure it would meet all of my needs and then some. I said to him, "this is much more than I will ever need or use." He said "that's o.k. it's there if you need it. By the way if you don't understand something just call me." That experience taught me a lot about purpose. It taught me that no one knows the full potential of a product like its creator. It also taught me that if I ever get to a point where I don't understand how it is supposed to work I can ask the creator and he will explain it to me. So it is with you and I. Whenever we get to the point of having to answer those five questions we must keep in mind that only God can answer them correctly. It is therefore imperative that every person come to establish a relationship with Jesus Christ the God of all creation.

In St. John 14:26 Jesus states, "But the Comforter, which is the Holy Ghost, whom the father will send in my name, **he shall teach you all things**, and bring all things to your remembrance, whatsoever I have said unto you." The scripture teaches that it is the purpose of the Holy Spirit to teach us. This includes teaching us about our purpose. The purpose of our individual lives is found in the mind of God who created us and the mind of God is accessed through the Holy Spirit. It is the Spirit of God that answers these five essential questions of life. When a believer is baptized in the Holy Spirit he now has access to the mind of God. It is through this relationship with the third in the trinity that we learn about our purpose. The Holy Spirit is the most important person on Earth. I love the names that Jesus calls the Holy Spirit. He refers to him as the Spirit of truth and as the Comforter. He calls him a leader and a guide and refers to him as a teacher and reminder of the things Jesus commanded and taught. With these various names we can see it is the Holy Spirit that brings us the revelation we need. If we have forgotten what Jesus has commanded the Holy Spirit is the one who reminds us. If we have lost our way it is the Holy Spirit that will guide us. If we are void of understanding it is the Holy Spirit that teaches us. If we are hurting it is the Holy Spirit that comforts us.

The Four characteristics we should know about the Holy Spirit is that he is:

1. The Spirit of Truth- the living Word in Spirit form.
2. He is the Comforter- God's very presence living in us.
3. He is the Teacher- Teaching us about God's purpose
4. He is our Leader and Guide- Going before us so we can follow.

Let's take a closer look at those five essential questions that every person must answer and some of the hindrances it may cause if we don't.

WHO AM I?

The first question we said was the question **"who am I?"** This question deals with our identity. When a person knows who they are it simplifies some of life's hardships. When I think about this subject I often think about Prince William the son of Prince Charles and the late Princess Diana. From his birth he has been told who he is and who his parents and grand parents are. I am certain that he grew up never having to second guess about his

35

royal status. From an early age he knew he was royalty. He also knew that because of his royal status he was afforded certain privileges. It is possible to have kingship states and royal privileges and not be aware of them. This is indeed the case with those who have not come to the knowledge of who they really are in Christ. When a person does not know who they are they will attempt to take on an identity that does not represent who they really are. How can you be something you are not? The answer is you can't. Have you ever seen celebrity impersonators? I use to wonder why they would give up their unique identity to take on the identity of someone else. I have since come to know that answer. To attempt to be someone else and take on their identity you cast away your own existence. Why be a second best carbon copy when you can be an original you?

Throughout the scriptures God is trying to tell us who we really are. It is only through a relationship with him can you ever know who you really are. If you have been struggling with the question of identity take a moment and read 1 Peter 2:9. Peter declares that we are (4) specific things in Christ. He says, "But you are a chosen generation, a royal priesthood, a holy nation, a peculiar people…" He goes on to explain why we are described this way. "That you should show forth the praises of him who has called you out of darkness into his marvelous light." This should give you a clear understanding that you are chosen, royalty (kings and priests), holy and peculiar in the family of God.

WHY AM I HERE?

The second question that must be answered is the question, **"why am I here?"** This question speaks directly about your purpose. Just like a coin purpose has two sides. Many of us are only aware of one side of the coin. The first side of the coin is found in the Word of God when Jesus instructs us to go and preach the gospel to every living creature and to make disciples of men (reference St. Mark 16:15). We call this the great commission. It is a vital part of our purpose. I also like to refer to this as our universal purpose. Every person has the same universal purpose. Many people ignore this universal purpose. In doing so, they ignore one half of their vital assignment in life. I believe that God uses this as a measuring stick to determine how much of your unique purpose he reveals to you. Your unique purpose is how you as an individual will go about accomplishing this. The more you are willing to participate in God's universal purpose the more you demonstrate that you can be trusted with the unique purpose. The more you participate in God's universal purpose the more your unique purpose is revealed. The end result of purpose is that the will of God be done. Your universal purpose as well as your unique purpose leads to others being ministered to and God receiving the glory from your obedience. I have little sayings that I call "cranisms." "Cranisms" can be original or borrowed. The cranism for purpose goes like this, "everything in life was created and made to benefit something outside of itself."

WHERE AM I FROM?

The third question that must be answered is the question, **"where am I from?"** This question has to do with heritage. The Old Testament makes up two thirds of the bible. In it God accounts for the heritage of man. He explains how man spread abroad on the earth and populated it. He even explains how important it was for the children of God to never forget their heritage. Understanding your heritage helps to give a person a sense of belonging. Heritage leads you back to your original source. God instructed the children of Isreal to always teach their children about their heritage. When I speak of heritage, I am not talking about the land of your nativity but instead about your origin. Where you originated from can only be answered by the creator. Where did it all begin? Heritage is so important to God that he documented not only the earthly birth of Jesus but he also documented his linage. His linage as well as ours leads back to God the source and sustainer of all mankind.

I was speaking to a friend the other day and asking questions about her family. We both concluded that neither of us could accurately track our families' history from both sides of our parents. The best that I was able to do was to name my grand parents and the best that she could do was to name her great grand parents. Obviously most of our ancestral history was lost with the migration of our people from Africa to America. From an education stand point this accounts for only the path that leads us back to our original place of nativity. The comfort that we must seek rests in the knowledge of His words concerning us. The word of God states in Genesis 1:27, "So God created man in his image, in the image of God created he him; male and female created he them." This passage of scripture tells me that even if I can not track my ancestral footsteps I can however rest in the assurance that those footsteps will ultimately lead me back to God. Where am I from? Is a powerful question with an equally powerful answer? In helping others find their way to Jesus is in essence helping them to find their way back to where they originated from. It is at that place of finding Jesus that we can answer that ever allusive question of where am I from?

WHAT CAN I DO?

The fourth question in human history that every person must answer is the question, **"what can I do?"** This question speaks of our potential. Potential is hidden strength, dormant power. It is what you can do but haven't done yet. It is what you can have but haven't obtained yet. It is what you can be but haven't become yet. And where you can go but haven't gone to yet. Potential is revealed when life makes demands on you that cause you to look deep inside and come up with a solution. This demand also requires you to do something that you have never done before to bring about the results you want. My cranism for potential is this: "If a man wants to become someone he has never been before he is going to have to do something he has never done before."

I was reading from a book by one of my favorite authors and he told a story about riding on a bus and passing a cemetery. As his mind began to wander and he thought about the lives that may have been led by those who were buried there. He heard the voice of the Lord say, that cemeteries are one of the richest plots of land there is. He understood later that the Lord was not referring to the nutrients in the soil or the lands value but instead was talking about the number of people who were buried there that had left this earth without fulfilling or living out their potential. He thought about all of the songs that had gone unsung and all of the books that had gone unwritten as well as all of the invention and creative ideas that had never been introduced to mankind. How often do we waste our potential because we are faced with a difficult task? How often do we settle for average when excellence is an option? I'm sure you have heard someone describe another in terms of their potential. As you have come to know through reading this book that no other product on earth can determine what another product can do. Only the creator of the product knows its true potential. The word of God also gives us a clear understanding of what we are capable of doing inside the scope of our calling and assignment in life. Philippians 4:13 says, "I can do all thing through Christ which strengthen me." This passage is very relevant when talking about our potential. Whenever a manufacturer builds a product he builds into the product everything it needs to accomplish its purpose. Without reading the owners' manual or consulting with the manufacturer you will never know what the full extent of the products potential is. The key to remember is that God has designed you and equipped you with everything you need to accomplish all that he has assigned you to accomplish. Before the foundation of the world your purpose was assigned to you. In assigning a purpose to you he equipped you with everything you need to get the job done. Yes, I know it may be hard for you to believe but everything you need is already inside you. The capacity to gain more knowledge is in you. The wisdom you seek is in you. The motivation you need to get started is in you. The determination you need to finish the task is in you. The creative idea you need to change your financial picture is also in you. To tap into the potential that is in you and to maximize that potential you must first come to know the one who gave you this hidden strength and untapped ability.

Potential is also a raw material. It must be shaped and made into a useful product whereby others can benefit from it. That creative idea has to be transformed into a workable commodity. That hidden strength or talent has to be cultivated and perfected in order to become a benefit to you. The capacity to learn more and to know more has to be challenged by new ideas and thoughts.

Once you have done something it is no longer your potential. It should no longer be viewed as a finished product or accomplishment but rather the beginning of discovering how much more of your potential can be accessed. Every challenge that you will face is an opportunity to reach inside and come up with the piece of potential that has never been used before. This is how the Creator has designed you.

WHERE AM I GOING?

The final question that every believer must answer is the question, **"where am I going?"** This question has to do with destiny. Destiny and purpose are so closely related that they resemble each other in almost every way. The distinct difference is purpose is the original intent for the existence of a thing and destiny is the course you travel to accomplish it. It is destiny and purpose that causes life to have meaning and fulfillment. It is purpose and destiny that keeps us moving forward because we believe we are on the right path to bring about God's plan for our life. When I think of destiny and the question, "where am I going?" I often think about the story of Joseph in the Bible. I often wondered what he must have been thinking when his dreams seemed to turn into a nightmare. I wonder did he question God at anytime. Did he wonder about the path that God had chosen for him? Whenever I am faced with the difficulties in life I am reminded that the footsteps of the righteous are ordered of the Lord. I am also reminded that those footsteps will often travel terrain that may not be comfortable for me. I am always assured that the path is indeed the one that God has chosen for me no matter how rough it may appear to be.

One of the most important questions concerning destiny is, are you on the right path? If the answer is yes, you can rest assured that you have the grace to handle any obstacle you may face. If the answer is no, take a moment and reevaluate where you are and where you want to go. Repent and ask the Holy Spirit to show you the right path. He is faithful and just to lead us if we allow it. It has always been and will always be God's intention that we seek Him for the answers to all of life's questions.

To All Fathers

When studying this principle on purpose I ask the Holy Spirit to teach me something unique about the principle. As I was studying the book of Proverbs chapter 22 I came across this familiar passage in verse 6. It reads, "Train up a child in the way he should go: and when he is old, he will not depart from it." The Holy Spirit then spoke and said, "This is a command concerning purpose. The statement "should go" is not an opinion but a clear narrative of direction." As He began to open my understanding and to give me revelation concerning the scripture it became crystal clear to me why this was a command to all fathers concerning their children. The understanding he gave me was that every father should be in such a committed relationship with Him and living by the word of God that God the Father will reveal to our natural fathers what the purpose of the child is. There are many scriptures in the Bible that back up this very revelation. However, the most prolific speaks of the birth and life of our savior Jesus. St. Matthew 1:20-21 says, "But while he thought on these things, behold, the angel of the Lord appeared unto him in a dream, saying, Joseph, thou son of David, fear not to take unto thee Mary thy wife: for that which is conceived in her is of the Holy Ghost. And she shall bring forth a son, and thou shalt call his name JESUS: for he shall save his people from their sins." This revelation warmed my heart. I immediately ask the Holy Spirit to reveal unto me the purpose of my daughter. Not only did He reveal her purpose to me He also gave me the name by which she would be called. Her name is Nia, which means purpose. What an awesome God! After receiving that revelation and understanding it has made raising this wonderful child such a joy. Knowing her purpose and sharing that purpose with her has been a source of peace and comfort for me and for her as well. Knowing purpose makes it easy to know when and what to say "yes" to.

Chapter 3

The Kingdom Principle of Purpose

Overview:

5 questions everyone must answer in life to help bring them to an understanding of God's purpose.

1. Who am I? (Identity)
2. Why am I here? (Purpose)
3. Where am I from? (Heritage)
4. What can I do? (Potential)
5. Where am I going? (Destiny)

Only God can answer these questions.

Until man seeks God and receives the answers to these life questions, his life has no significance or meaning.

To All Fathers

CHAPTER 4

The Kingdom Principle of a Solid Foundation

"He is like a man which built a house, and digged deep, and laid the foundation on a rock: and when the flood arose, the stream beat vehemently upon that house, and could not shake it: for it was founded upon a rock." St. Luke 6:48

I have never had to experience what it is like to lose a child. I can only imagine the hurt a parent must feel to lose such a significant part of you. As I was standing in line to pay my respects to my co worker and friend I was reminded of what it really means to have your life founded on a rock. I watched him as he greeted each one of the visitors with the same genuine smile. Even though we were there to pay our respects and to console him and his family he was more concerned with making each one of us feel comfortable in and uncomfortable situation. He leaned over and hugged me and thanked me for coming. I asked, "How are you?" He said, "Just fine." He shared a few more pleasantries and embraced me once again before moving on to the next guest. While driving home I thought about what an amazing man of God. Even at what seemed to be one of his darkest moments he was still serving others. At a time when no one would blame him for wanting everyone to be concerned about him and his family he was demonstrating what it means to have your life founded on Jesus.

Not Shaken by the Storm

As believers in the Kingdom of God we are instructed to dig deep and build our lives on the Rock which is Jesus. It is our responsibility to grow in the knowledge of Him. Encountering storms is a part of our faith walk. The significance of the storm and its ability to harm you depends mostly on you. When building a house the most important part of the building process takes place when you are laying the foundation. It is the foundation that supports everything else that will be built on it. The roof of the house is important as well as the walls that will enclose it but of the three the foundation is the most important. Without a solid foundation the roof and walls have no real support. In the Word of God the bible teaches us that we are considered wise if we hear the words and instructions of Jesus and do them. He says to us that when we hear the Word of God, understand the Word of God, believe the Word of God and become doers of the Word of God we can face the storms of life and they won't even shake us because we are founded on the principles of the Kingdom. Jesus teaches us that it is not the magnitude of the storms in life that causes our lives to fall but rather what our lives are founded on. When a storm rises in your life are you looking for a practice used by the world or are you looking for the principle of the Kingdom of God that applies to your situation? To have a solid foundation you must become a student of the Word of God through hearing the Word, understanding the Word, believing the Word and then applying the Word of God. This is the only way a solid foundation can be built.

Why the Storms of Life Come

I have heard over the years that you shouldn't ask God why. I'm here to tell you that it is not the will of God that you are ignorant of the knowledge that God has provided through his Word and Sprit. It is imperative that the believer know and understand why the storms of life come and how to overcome them using the Word of God.

There are (4) reason why we experience storms in life. It is vital that the believer know and understand these reasons. Once you have identified why the storm is there you can then apply the correct principle to overcome the storm. Remember it is God's will that we overcome all of the challenges we face in life by the faith of Jesus Christ. Let's identify all (4) reasons for the storm and then discuss and explain each one individually. Storms come for these reasons:

1. Human Error
2. Challenges of the Times
3. Satanic Attack
4. The call of God

Human Error

Satan is the influencer of evil thoughts. However he is not the reason we commit sin. It is possible to willfully choose sin over righteousness. Jesus knew this and that's why he offers forgiveness through his blood. The first reason storms come into our life is because of human error or sin. The Bible says that we make mistakes for only two reasons: we don't know the scriptures nor do we know the power of God. (Matthew 22:29) Storms caused by human error can be a direct result of our disobedience to the Word of God. It is inevitable that we will experience the negative consequences of sin and willful disobedience to the Word of God.

Many people fail to realize the importance of obeying God and continue down the path of sin. They believe that if there is no immediate discomfort or interruption in their plans that there must not be consequences associated with their actions. The scripture concludes that the wages of sin is death. In this case the Word says that the payment for sin is separation from God who is our source and sustainer. Just like working a job where you receive your paycheck weekly or semi-monthly the wages of sin can be accrued and built up over time. Just like the hours you accumulate on your job so it is with sin that has gone unforgiven and unrepentant of. It has been accruing over time. The longer you wait to acknowledge your wrong the greater the repayments for those consequences will be. There is no sin that man can commit that will not be addressed by the Father. It is unfortunate that we fail to realize the impact of willful sin and the participation in it. Paul tells Timothy in 1 Timothy 5:24 that, "Some men's sins are open beforehand, going before to judgment; and some men they follow after." He explains that no matter what the sin it will either be dealt with swiftly because it is open and obvious or it may be prolonged because they are less open but this will also be dealt with as well.

How to Stop This Storm

Many who are experiencing the storm caused by their own human error can come out of the storm by simply repenting of their sins. Once you have repented the storm ceases to exist. You must also remember that the longer you wait to repent the more destructive damage the storm does. The damage caused by the storm determines the effort required to rebuild after the storm.

I want to explain the true definition of repentance and show the (4) steps required by God to determine whether repentance has taken place. I will also point out what God will do for the believer once repentance has taken place. When I was a young man just starting my walk with God I heard my mentor teach on the subject of forgiveness. He reiterates the story found in Matthew 18:21, 22 which states, "Then came Peter to him, and said, Lord, how often shall my brother sin against me, and I forgive him? Till seven times? Jesus said unto him, I say not unto thee, until seven times: but, until seventy times seven." He also said that God will forgive my sins no matter how many times I commit them. My first thought to my ignorance and shame was not what a loving God we have, but that I could continue to sin forever as long as I asked God to forgive me. Shortly after that during one of our many conversations I asked him about what he had said about my dilemma. He calmly explained to me that there was a distinct difference between asking for forgiveness and repentance. The true understanding of repentance is found in 2 Chronicles 7:14 a very familiar passage of scripture. It states, "If my people, who are called by name shall humble themselves and pray, and seek my face, and turn from their wicked ways; then will I hear from heaven, and will forgive their sins, and will heal their lands." Notice in the scripture that there are (4) specific things that is required by God that we as believers must do in order to repent. The first step is that we must humble ourselves. This means that we must become teachable and submissive to God's word, his will and his way. The second thing that is required is we must pray. Prayer is our verbal invitation to get God involved in the situation. The third thing is to seek His face. Notice the scripture does not say that we should seek his hand but rather his face. This denotes that there must be a willingness to know Him intimately. The final thing is we must then turn from our wicked ways. Often times when repentance is taught it is taught as just turning away from the committed act of sin. Remember the turning away is just the fourth and final step of true repentance. The other three steps must be done first and in order. After these four things have been done, God then says He will hear from heaven, and will forgive your sins, and will heal your lands. In this case of repentance the land also represents the heart of man. He will heal your heart. What an incredible God we serve!

In the book of Genesis chapter 2 verses 17 God gives the man his instructions concerning the tree of the knowledge of good and evil. He tells the man, "But of the tree of the knowledge of good and evil, thou shall not eat of it: for in the day that thou eat thereof thou shall surely die." You may say that once he ate he didn't immediately die. Physically his soul and spirit did not exit his body which is what physical death is; he did however die spiritually. He was at that very moment separated from God. By Adam being the first man all of mankind preceded from him. It was that act of disobedience that separated all of mankind from God. Also know that the seed of death entered his physical body as well. From that moment on their physical bodies began to age and break down. Not immediately but gradually over time until it returned to the dust from where it came. Adam's sin and disobedience causes a spiritual death (separation) and caused our physical bodies to be subject to deterioration over time. Human error caused by my own actions must be repented of to cause this storm to stop.

Human Error Caused by Others

It is possible to be caught up in a storm that you didn't cause or create through your own sin or disobedience. I often think about those who were on the ship with Jonah and were caught up in the storm because of Jonah's disobedience. (Jonah 1:12-13) "And he said unto them, Take me up, and cast me forth into the sea; so shall the sea be calm unto you: for I know that for my sake this great tempest is upon you." Nevertheless the men rowed hard to bring it to the land; but they could not: for the sea wrought and was tempestuous against them." Take head when you see someone who is in continued disobedience to the will of God. It is possible to get caught up in their storm. If you find yourself in that situation you must forgive them. Once you have forgiven them for their part in the storm you can go free and the storm no longer has power over you. If you do not forgive you remain in the storm with them and will eventually feel the great devastation that is accruing over time against them.

How to Stop This Storm

Remember if the storm was caused by your disobedience you must repent in order to cause the storm to cease. If the storm was caused by others and you are being effected you must forgive them. Once you have forgiven them the storm ceases for you and you can then go free.

Challenges of the Times

One of my thoughts when I witnessed the devastation of Hurricane Katrina was how many believers were caught up in this natural storm. As I watched the news casts and read reports of the total disaster the region faced I was reminded of Psalm 34:19. It says, "Many are the afflictions of the righteous: but the Lord delivers him out of them all." It has been a misconception that believers are somehow exempt from the challenges of life. It only takes watching a disaster like Katrina to remind us that even those who are called of God are not exempt from this type of storm.

In the book of 1 Kings 17 the Word of God tells about the prophet Elijah and his command to go and hide himself by the brook of Cherith. God told him that he would get his water from the brook and that He had commanded the ravens to feed him daily. In verse 7 the Word of God says, "And it came to pass after a while, that the brook dried up, because there had been no rain in the land. Here Elijah was faced with a situation that was beyond his control.

There was no more water at the brook to sustain him. Verse 8-9 says, "And the word of the Lord came unto him saying, Arise get thee to Zarephath which belongs to Zidon, and dwell there: behold I have commanded a widow woman there to sustain thee."

The principle understanding here that must be observed is when your resources are exhausted because of the challenges of the times you must listen to the instructions of the Lord who will tell you immediately what to do and where to go. Imagine what would have happened had Elijah stayed at the brook. I believe he would have eventually died of thirst and accused God of not caring. Whenever you are facing this type of storm that is beyond your control remember Psalms 34:19. "Many are the afflictions of the righteous: but the Lord delivers him out of them all." Notice that God spoke to him and told him that He had already commanded a widow woman to sustain him. God has already mapped out your course in life and has already commanded those who are to assist you along the way. The success of overcoming this type of storm lies in your sensitivity to the voice of God and your willingness to obey and follow His plan of action.

How to Stop This Storm

The key to coming out of this storm is your ability to recognize and be sensitive to the voice of the Holy Spirit. The primary way that God will deliver you is by giving you a plan of action. To come out of the storm you must be obedient to His plan.

Satanic Attacks

The third reason we face storms in life is because of satanic attacks. Satan does not have the power to cause us to sin he can only influence our decisions to sin. The plan of God for our life does not include sin and is not and never has been a part of God's design for mankind. Satan through his suggestive influence must convince us that to disobey God will somehow bring us a greater sense of value. In the lives of ignorant believers Satan has the power to convince them through perverting the Word of God that his way is better than God's.

Made to Play by the Rules

One of the first recorded satanic attacks takes place in the book of Job. Job, because of his limited understanding was a pawn in a spiritual chess game between God and Satan. God asked Satan a question in the book of Job 1:7. "And the Lord said unto Satan, Whence cometh thou? Then Satan answered the Lord and said, from going to and fro in the earth, and from walking up and down in it." To stop Satan's bragging God asked him if he had considered his servant Job. Satan replied that he knew him and that he was aware of how God has protected him from any attacks. Satan told God that if he were allowed to attack Job he would make him curse God to his face. Of course we know how the challenge ends.

The most important principle to learn here is that Satan is limited in his ability through God's protection to attack you. He must first gain permission from God to engage a child of God who is walking in righteousness before God. Satan has all jurisdictions in all areas of darkness. This is why it is so vitally important that we live according to the principles of the Kingdom of God. Satan must obey God's rule concerning his children. The rule is found in 1 Corinthians 10:13. It says, "There hath no temptation taken you but such is common to man: but God is faithful, who will not suffer (allow) you to be tempted (tested) above that which you are able: but will with the temptation also make a way to escape, that you may be able to bear it." The wonderful thing to remember here is that if you are experiencing an attack from Satan; God trusts that you have the understanding and power in you to handle it.

What is a Satanic Attack?

A satanic attack is anything that comes against your willingness and desire to obey the will of God. This includes all things spiritual, mental, and physical that will serve as an obstacle to the plan of God. The judgment of Satan was executed before the creation of mankind. His fate has been sealed, his future already determined and his days numbered. This was all accomplished by our Lord and Savior Jesus. The keys of the kingdom which represents authority and the rightful ownership of the earth have been given to Jesus. He in turn reclaimed the kingdom for us and gave to us the keys of the kingdom. St. Luke 10:19 declares, "Behold, I give unto you power to tread on serpents and scorpions, and over all the power of the enemy: and nothing shall by any means hurt you." God has assured us that Satan does not have the ability to hurt the children of God if we understand our spiritual authority and use it. Jesus said that he has given us power over all the power of the enemy. Once you recognize the power you possess through the Holy Spirit you can begin to walk in your God given authority. In any satanic attack you must remember that you have the power and authority over all the power of the enemy.

A Strong Rebuke

In Luke chapter 8: 22-25 it tells us of the time when Jesus quieted the storm. In verse 22 Jesus says to his disciples, "Let us go to the other side of the lake." When Jesus made this declaration we know that the will of God was for them to make it to the other side of the lake. In the process of doing the will of God a storm came down on the lake and the boat was filled with water and they were in jeopardy. As Jesus slept the disciples were afraid and came and woke him and said, "Master, master we parish." Verse 24 says, "Then he rose, and rebuked the wind and the raging of the water: and they ceased, and there was a calm." I want you to notice that Jesus rebuked the winds and the waves. The word rebuke means to declare unlawful. Jesus declared that the storm in the form of the winds and the waves was unlawful. It wasn't supposed to be there. In another passage of scripture it is recorded that Jesus said to the storm, "peace be still" and it obeyed Him. Notice here that Jesus told the storm what it was supposed to be (peaceful and still). Anything that comes to hinder the will of God from coming to pass in your life is unlawful and must be rebuked. After the storm ceased Jesus turns to his disciples and asked them, "Where is your faith?" In other words he asked them, "Why didn't you do it?" Where are your understanding, belief and application of this kingdom principle? Jesus was telling them had they applied the same principle the winds and the waves would have obeyed them also. As a believer the same applies to us. Many of us are experiencing satanic attacks and are crying out to God to stop the storm and just like Jesus did with his disciples he is trying to get us to understand that we have the power to declare the storm unlawful ourselves. Taking authority over Satan and the storm is the believers right as a kingdom child. What areas are you experiencing a storm? Is it your marriage, your finances, your career, your children or your faith walk with God? Whenever Satan comes to hinder the plan and will of God from coming to pass in your life he must be rebuked. Take a moment and think of the areas that you are experiencing a storm and rebuke Satan now in the name of Jesus. Speak to your situation and tell the conditions that are contrary to what they should be what you expect. This is what Jesus did when He spoke to the conditions of the storm, the winds and the waves, and told them how they should be. He simply said, "Peace, be still." And the winds ceased and there was a great calm. (St. Mark 4:39) The same power that dwells in our Lord and Savior now dwells in you. Remember you have both the power and authority in Jesus name to rebuke all the storms in your life caused by satanic attack. You do not however have the authority to rebuke him if you are bowing down to him through the participation in his sinful activities. In other words you cannot command the one you are serving.

The Call of God

The fourth reason storms come is because of the call of God on our lives. I was reminded that there can be no victories won unless there are battles fought.

Ministry as a whole is a way of life for many. I have come to learn first hand that when you step out of your fear and begin to obey God storms will come. The greater the call on your life the greater the storms you face. The wonderful part about that is the principles to overcome the storms remain the same. Just like a student learning the principles of mathematics, the numbers may increase in size but as long as the student knows and understands the principle it doesn't matter how large the numbers become they can still work the principle. It may take longer to execute because of the size of the numbers but the principle to solve the problem never changes.

One day David ventured out to the battle field and witnessed a giant Philistine threatening the army of God. It was very clear that all of the military men of God's army were afraid and feared for their lives. As David inquired of his brothers he found that no man was willing to face the Philistine. When David approached Saul the King he asked for the opportunity to face the giant in battle. Unlike the others who were trained soldiers David was a sheppard a keeper of his father's sheep. As David listened to the giant curse the people of God and defy God's army he became angry. Unlike the others David was not afraid. There was a king growing up on the inside. It was the call of God on his life that lead him to the battle field that day. It was the call of God that allowed him to face the giant and it was the call of God that caused him to triumph over the giant.

When facing a storm caused by the call of God you will experience great faith and courage. The confidence of knowing you were called for that particular purpose will be evident in both your words and your actions. Victory for you has already happened.

God's Intentions

It has always been God's intention to get you where he needs you to be to become who he really knows you are. It is in these situations that God knows that you are both equipped and willing to go through the storm. The storms that are caused by the call of God are not like other storms. This storm is one that you must simply ride out. There are 4 key reasons why it is so important that you recognize this kind of storm. They are as follows:

1. You cannot rebuke God and must accept that this is part of His calling for your life.
2. To reveal to the world through you that the promises of God are at work in your life. To build on your faith through a victorious outcome.
3. God has someone watching you. You are serving as a contemporary model for Him at this time to demonstrate how to overcome the challenges of the storm.
4. God is more interested in your development then He is your deliverance. It is His intention to build the character in you to function in the capacity that brings Him the most glory.

We as believer over look this most important principle. We fail to realize sometimes that others will gain a greater understanding of God's purpose and power from watching us.

It was Jesus love and commitment to the Father and His call that led Him to the cross.

Remember challenges will come because of the call of God on our lives. He has called us to be like Him which also includes suffering. The Word of God says, "Though he was a Son, yet learned he obedience by the things which he suffered." (Hebrews 5:8) 1Peter 2:21 also states, "For even hereunto you were called: because Christ also suffered for us, leaving us an example, that you should follow his steps." This must be our mind set also.

Chapter 4

The Kingdom Principle of a Solid Foundation

Overview

The foundation God intends all of us to build on is the Word of God. (Jesus Christ)

Why do storms come?

(4) Reasons storms come:

- Human Error
- The Challenges of the Times
- Satanic Attacks
- The Call of God

Each storm has a unique application to cause them to cease.

- Human Error caused by you/ Repentance
- Human Error caused by others/ Forgiveness
- Challenges of the Times/ God's Instructions
- Satanic Attacks/ A strong rebuke
- The Call of God/ Ride it out

CHAPTER 5

The Kingdom principle of Sowing and Reaping

"Be not deceived; God is not mocked: for whatsoever a man soweth, that shall he also reap." Galatians 6:7

My office building is located on a highway surrounded by corn fields. It was an unusually hot afternoon with lots of humidity. We were all struggling to keep cool by remaining inside. One of the other salesman said, "That corn will grow another foot by tomorrow." I was amazed already at how fast it had grown and how tall it had gotten. Many of the tallest trucks which stand about 8 feet seemed to be short in comparison to the corn peeping over the top of it. As I gazed out the window from my desk the Spirit of the Lord spoke to me and said, "Go out to the corn field." When I arrive at the back of the building I could see the beautiful corn stalks and its budding ears. I remembered thinking how pleased the farmers would be at harvest time. The Lord instructed me to pick one of the ears of corn and look at it. As I picked the ear and pulled back the layers to expose the corn, I was in awe with what I saw. The Spirit of God said, "If you understand this principle and apply it you will always be fruitful." When I came inside to ponder what was said the revelation of this truth came to me. One ear of corn had over 450 cornels. One seed had multiplied into over 450 seeds just like the one that had been planted.

In the Kingdom of God a seed is any word you say, any action you do or thought you think. The principle says, any word said or action performed is a seed sown and once it is sown a harvest is guaranteed. The Word of God tells us that we have the ability to sew both spiritually as well as naturally. Galatians 6:8 indicates, "For he who sows to his flesh shall of the flesh reap corruption; but he that sows to the Spirit shall of the Spirit reap life everlasting." Sowing to the flesh means to conduct oneself by the evil dictates and desires of the sinful nature of man, thus practicing the deeds of the flesh. Those deeds are found in Galatians 5:19-21 it reads as follows: "Now the works of the flesh are manifest, which are these; adultery, fornication, uncleanness, lasciviousness, idolatry, witchcraft, hatred, variance, emulations, wrath, strife, seditions, heresies, envying, murders, drunkenness, revelings, and such like: of the which I tell you before, as I have told you in time past, that they which do such things shall not inherit the kingdom of God." According to the principle of the Word of God these seeds will return unto the sower a multiplied harvest that will keep them from their inheritance which is the kingdom of God. The second half of the promise found in Galatians 6:8 says," but he that sows to the Spirit shall of the Spirit reap life everlasting." This means to live by the Holy Spirits enabling help which prompts us and leads us into all truth and righteousness, thus cultivating the fruit of the Spirit found in Galatians 5:22-23. Such a person shall reap life everlasting, that is, to be rewarded with eternal life with Christ.

In each case, whether we are sowing to the flesh or to the Spirit we are planting seeds that will return to us a harvest. The question that is most important is what kind of harvest do you want? If it is a life of destruction than we can continue to sow to our flesh, but if you are seeking life and its abundance and eternal life with Christ than sowing to the Spirit will be your choice.

(4) Phases of Sowing Your Seeds

Before sowing your seed there are (4) things to consider. The application of this process is the key to understanding how the seed principle works.

Determine what type of harvest you want.

We can better understand this principle by looking at the natural application first. When a farmer wants corn he plants a corn seed. When he wants beans he plants a bean seed and when he wants wheat he plants a wheat seed. The spiritual application is the same as the natural application. It states that the spiritual application can and will produce for us the natural manifestation. Remember a seed is any thought you think, any words you say or action you do. Therefore if I want more friends I must sow the seed of friendship. Proverbs 18:24 says, "A man that has friends must show himself friendly." When I want forgiveness I must sow the seed of forgiveness. Mark 11:25 states, "And when you stand praying forgive, if you have aught against any: that your Father also which is in heaven may forgive your trespasses." When I want to increase my faith I must sow the Word of God continually in my heart. When I want finances I must sow a financial seed that will bring about the harvest I desire. I will discuss the financial seed and its application later in the chapter.

Determine what kind of seed to plant.

The out come of the harvest for your life can be orchestrated by the seeds you sow. Seeds are already pre programmed to reproduce after its kind. An apple seed cannot produce oranges neither can a hate seed produce love. Each seed created by God can only reproduce what its original nature is. Genesis 1:11 says, "And God said, Let the earth bring forth grass, the herb yielding seed, and the fruit tree yielding fruit after its kind, whose seed is in itself, upon the earth: and it was so." With this understanding we can order the kind of harvest we desire with our seeds. A part of our experiences are a direct result of the seeds we have sown both good and evil. Whatever you are currently experiencing in life it is the result of the seeds you have sown in the past. God has given us the power to dictate the kind of harvest we want to be produced in life. With this authority it is up to us to plant the kind of seeds that will bring the harvest we intend. The kinds of seeds you plant and the harvest you receive from it is strictly up to you.

Determine how much of a harvest you want.

The size of your harvest is determined by how much you plant. That is strictly up to you. Remember that the seed planted will multiply and return to you multiple seeds just like the one you planted. God tells us that if we sow sparingly we will also reap sparingly but if we sow bountifully we will reap bountifully. It sounds as if God allows us to choose our harvest size. Many people violate this principle by not sowing enough of what they want from the beginning. For example, if both you and I are farmers and we both decided to plant corn in our fields and you decided to plant 100 rows of corn and I decided to plant only 50 rows of corn when harvest time comes and you have more corn I shouldn't be upset with you because we both determined what we wanted our harvest to be when we planted. In your situation you received more at harvest time because you were willing to sacrifice more at the beginning for a greater return later. I have often said that many people trade what they want most for what the want at the moment. In doing so we miss out on the tremendous harvest we could have had; had we sacrificed more at the first for a greater return at harvest time.

Make sure the soil is ready to receive the seed.

The most important phase of sowing and reaping is this phase. The soil must be ready to receive the seed. By using the natural application the farmer knows he must spend countless hours in the field preparing the soil. He must remove any and all foreign objects that will hinder the seeds growth and development. He must also fertilize the soil and make sure it has the right nutrients in it to allow the seed to grow. Jesus explained this principle to his disciples in Matthew 13:19-23. Jesus explains that the soil represents the heart of man. This is very important because the condition of your heart will determine what happens to the seed. When your heart is full of bitterness and unforgivness the seed cannot grow. When your heart is filled with the cares of this world the seed cannot grow. When the heart does not understand what it has received the seed cannot grow. It is so vitally important that we understand this principle of the kingdom of God. In the book of Mark 4:13 Jesus says to his disciples after teaching about the parable of the sower, "And he said unto them, Know ye not this parable? And how then will you know all parables?" Jesus said this in reference to the Kingdom of God. He was saying to them if you don't understand this principle doubtless will you be able to understand any of the kingdom principles.

It is the content of the heart that determines whether the seeds you have planted will grow. A good seed cannot grow in corrupt and contaminated soil. It is up to us to make sure the soil is ready to receive the seed. One of my mentors faith confessions is lord don't allow anything to get hung up in my spirit. He understands that the condition of his heart will determine his harvest. It is safe to say again that what we are currently experiencing in our lives is a product of the seeds we have sown. If you are experiencing the wonderful attributes of the Spirit continue to sow those seeds. Galatians 5:22-23 gives us the fruit of the Spirit. Genesis tells us that the fruit has its seed in itself. Therefore if we sow the seeds that are listed in Galatians 5:22-23 (love, joy, peace, long suffering, gentleness, goodness, faith, meekness and temperance.) they will reproduce after itself.

The Money Seed

It is my sincere prayer that there is a complete revelation concerning this application of the principle of sowing and reaping. When the

Lord explained this application to me it was with the understanding that the greatest way God will test your faith is through your giving. Giving is the greatest expression of love there is. Jesus said in St. John 15:13, "Greater love hath no man than this that a man lay down his life for his friends." St John 3:16 says, "For God so loved the world that he gave his only begotten Son, that whosoever believes in him shall not perish, but has everlasting life." What an incredible expression of love!

As I stated earlier there is both a natural application and a spiritual application to sowing and reaping, just as there is with every kingdom principle of God. The money seed is a unique kind of seed. The Word of God teaches that every seed is preprogrammed to reproduce after its own kind. However, the money seed is the only seed God allows you to name. At my local church we teach the giver to never plant a seed (give an offering) with out naming that seed. The money seed is the only seed that is not preprogrammed from the beginning. It requires that the believer give it an assignment. Tell God what it's for. There are two very powerful examples in the bible that supports this incredible principle. Abram was chosen of God to be the father of many nations. It was through the promised seed that came through his linage that we are able to enjoy a relationship with God today. One night as Abram was talking with God the Lord told him that he would be the father of many nations. God had him to look up at the night sky and said, "look now toward heaven, and tell the stars, if thou be able to number them: and he said unto him so shall your seed be." Genesis 15:7 states this, "And he said unto him, I am the Lord that brought thee out of Ur of the Chaldees, to give thee this land to inherit it." Abram then said to God in verse 8, "where by shall I know I shall inherit it?" Abram ask God to give him an understanding of how he would be able to know the promise of God was to come to pass. The next statement from God is incredible. God says to Abram give me an offering. God instructed Abram to give a certain offering and after that he would reveal to him how this was to be. Abram named his seed and God granted his request. The second application is found in the book of II Chronicles 1: 6-12. Solomon the king offered up to God a thousand burnt offerings and in doing so activated this kingdom principle. God came to Solomon in the night and said unto him, "Ask what I shall give thee. And Solomon said unto God, Thou hast showed great mercy unto David my father and hast made me to reign in his stead. Now, O Lord God, let thy promise unto David my father be established: for thou hast made me king over a people like the dust of the earth in multitude. Give me wisdom and knowledge that I may go out and come in before this people: for who can judge this thy people so great?" God granted Solomon's request. When Solomon sowed his offering God asked him what he wanted because Solomon didn't indicate what it was for when he sowed it. God gave him an opportunity to participate in the principle of sowing and reaping. What an awesome principle.

Many of God's people have been giving and sowing for quite some time and have not seen any significant changes in their situations. I challenge you to name the next seed you sow and watch God answer according to this principle.

Think of it in the natural sense. A farmer would never plant a seed into the ground and not expect a harvest. That is the sole reason he plants the seed, he wants the seed to return a harvest back to him. This principle works exactly the same way in the spirit as it does in the natural. Unfortunately there are many children of God who don't understand this principle and continue to give offerings with no real purpose. They continue to live beneath their privilege without an understanding of why and this is one of the reasons. The principle has been violated but not broken.

For all of you who have sown seeds in the past and have not named them or told God what it was for I have some wonderful news for you. A seed sown into the kingdom of God never loses its value. It is still waiting for you to give it an assignment. One of the wonderful things about God is he will never allow you to support his earthly cause without giving you a reward for doing so. Take a moment and think of all the offerings you have given in the past. Then take a moment and ask God is there any thing in the soil of your heart that will prohibit that seed from growing. If so ask the Lord to forgive you and repent of those sins and watch what the seed produces for you.

I have practiced this principle for years now and I can attest to the fact that God's principles are true. I was in an incredible legal contractual battle that seemingly was out of my control. I was in a position to have to prove my innocence in a situation. A few weeks before the court date I began to seek God's face. I asked the Lord to show me what I needed to vindicate myself from this wrongful accusation. When I prayed I stayed there to listen for an answer. After staying on my knees for quite some time I rose to my feet and walked over to my television set and turned it to TBN. They were in the midst of there yearly telethon. The host of the program said, "Some of you watching right now have been watching for years and the program has been a blessing to you, yet you have never contributed to the ministry." At that moment I said to the Lord, "if you will show me the way through this situation I will send them a check for $1000.00 dollars first thing in the morning." As soon as I finished getting that statement out of my mouth the Spirit of the Lord spoke and said, "Send them $2000.00." The next morning I went to the bank and got a cashier check and sent it off without hesitation. Later that day I received from my attorney's office a copy of the records from my accusers. As I flipped through the paperwork I came across an internal document that only the company uses for its in house records. This was the document I needed. Soon after, we went to court and produced this document and it was the exact piece I needed.

My pastor and mentor gave one of the most incredible testimonies concerning this principle I have ever heard. During a time we call impact giving he recited this testimony. One evening during a service he was preparing to give in the offering. At that moment he heard the Spirit of God say to him, "Name your seed." He said to the congregation that he had heard this principle taught before but had never preached about it himself. He indicated that he really didn't know how he felt about it. However, what he did know was the voice of the Lord. As he got his seed in his hand he told the Lord that this seed would be for his brother's salvation. His older brother had backslidden from the church for 17 years and was heavily entrenched in drugs. He sowed that seed that night and within seven days his brother came walking through the doors of the church and gave his life back to the Lord. He has been preaching the gospel of Jesus Christ ever since. Wow! How awesome is that? I am fully persuaded that all of the principles of

God work. The principle of sowing and reaping is not complete until you receive the harvest you intended once you have named your seed.

II Corinthians 9:7 states, "Every man according as he purposes in his heart, so let him give." This statement not only means to give what you choose to give but also to give with a specific purpose.

(4) Things God does for a Sower

It is God who gives seed to the sower according to II Corinthians 9:10. It is possible to be church goers and not be a sower. It is possible to be a choir member and not be a sower. It is possible to be a deacon and not be a sower. It is possible to be an apostle, prophet, pastor, teacher and evangelist (however not an effective one) and not be a sower. God only promises to give seed to the sower. There are four things that God does for the sower. They are as follows:

Makes all grace abound toward you

II Corinthians 9:8 says, "And God is able to make all grace abound toward you; that you, always having all sufficiency in all things may abound to every good work." This wonderful scripture means that God has the ability to cause others to use their gifts, talents and resources to help you. God even explains why He will do this and what the increase should be used for. He says, "Always having all sufficiency (more than enough) in all things may abound to every good work." This means we will have more than enough to contribute to every good cause of Christ.

Gives you sufficiency for your own needs

Verse 10 of II Corinthians says, "Now he that ministers seeds to the sower, both minister bread for your food," God will always make sure that the sower has more than enough for his own needs to be met. This is God's commitment to the sower.

He multiplies your seed sown

Verse 10 states, "Now he that ministers seed to the sower both minister bread for your food, and multiply your seed sown." Just like the ear of corn that started with one cornel, God multiplies it. In its broad perspective if you were holding an apple seed in your hand potentially you would be holding an orchard. If you were holding a grape seed in your hand you would potentially be holding a vineyard. If you were holding a money seed in your hand potentially you would be holding a fortune. God multiplies your seed sown.

He increases the fruit of your righteousness

"Now he that ministers seed to the sower both minister bread for your food, and multiply your seed sown, and increase the fruits of your righteousness." The wonderful reality of this promise is that as we sow our seed God will increase the fruits of our righteousness. You ask what does that mean. Galatians 5: 22-23 tells us of the 9 fruits of the Spirit. God will increase our love, joy, peace, long suffering, gentleness, goodness, faith, meekness and temperance. What an incredible commitment to the sower.

Take a moment and examine yourself and quietly ask God what kind of seed should you sow and what should be the purpose of that seed. When you do this with a clean heart and a cheerful attitude your seed will grow and multiply.

Prepare yourself to see an incredible increase because of the seeds you have already sown. If you have been one of those who did not fully understand this principle and now can see its truth, take a moment and make a list of the things you desire and name those seeds accordingly. Prepare to receive the harvest just as God intended. What an incredible principle!

Chapter 5

The Kingdom Principle of Sowing and Reaping

Overview

A seed is any words you say, any action you do or thought you think.

The heart of man is the soil that the seed is planted in.

(4) Things to consider when sowing your seed

- Determine what type of harvest you want
- Determine what type of seed you need to plant
- Determine how much of a harvest you want
- Make sure the soil is ready to receive the seed

The Money Seed (The only seed that is not preprogrammed)

(4) Things God does for a sower

- Makes all grace abound toward you
- Gives you sufficiency for your own needs
- He multiplies your seed sown
- He increases the fruits of your righteousness

CHAPTER 6

The Kingdom Principle of Potential

"....every branch that bears fruit he purges it that it may bring forth more fruit" St John 15:2

I am a huge basketball fan especially, the professional game. Michael Jordan is my all time favorite. When the Chicago Bulls would play I would make it a point to adjust my schedule to be able to watch or listen to every game. He so captivated me with the things he could do on the basketball court that I was truly saddened when he announced his first retirement. I remember feeling this pit in the middle of my stomach. It felt like a huge ball was just sitting there. I later realized I was not the only basketball fan that felt that way. There is something to be said about a person who can do the things they do in such excellence and make it look effortless and natural. I loved the fact that he was a winner and was willing to use all that he had been given to accomplish his dream of being a great repeat champion. We were privileged to be able to witness such an incredible talent. During an acceptance ceremony for one of his NBA Most Valuable Player Awards David Stern the commissioner of the league before presenting him with the award had these words to say. As he reeled off his many accomplishments he said, "You are simply the standard by which basketball excellence is measured" The statement was a great compliment. I remember thinking where he had come from. Being cut from his high school basketball team must have awakened a desire in him to become who he knew he could be. Somewhere deep inside he decided to make a demand on his potential. Thank God he did.

Potential is hidden strength and untapped ability. It is what is lying dormant inside you. It's what you can do but haven't done yet. It is what you can be but haven't become yet. It is where you can go but haven't gone yet and it is what you can have but haven't obtained yet. Potential is raw material. It is the creative substance that is used to make things.

The Make up of Man

Man kind is a triune being. We are comprised of three parts. We are spirit, we live in a physical body and we possess a soul. The spirit part of man is the part that is most like God. Jesus said, "God is a Spirit" (St. John 4:24) When man was created God chose to use the same material that He is. It is the spirit of man that longs for God's presence. It is the spirit man that hears the voice of God when He speaks and it is the spirit of man that Jesus came to save. The part that is most like God is your spirit. We also live in a physical body which has the appearance of life because the spirit is in it. Just as I gave the example earlier in the previous chapter, think of the body as a glove and your hand as your human spirit. As long as the hand is in the glove the glove appears to have life. However, the moment the hand is removed from the glove the glove falls lifelessly to the ground. So it is with us, as long as the spirit is inside the body the body appears to be alive. Physical death is simply the separation of the soul and spirit from the body. We also possess a soul. The soul of man is generally classified as his mind. This is true; however I would like to expand the soul to include the mind as well as the other components the mind controls. The soul of man has (5) components. They are the mind, will, imagination, emotions and intellect. These five components make up the soul of man.

It is in this area that I want to focus on the kingdom principle of potential. When the bible speaks of the flesh it is not always talking about your outward covering or skin. It is also talking about the unregenerate soul of man, the part that is at war with your spirit. It has always been God's will that we be led by the Spirit of God and not follow the dictates of the flesh. Paul writes in Philippians 4:13, "I can do all things through Christ who strengthens me." Paul indicates that he can do what God intended because it is God who strengthens him. Here, we are able to understand clearly that it is God who gives strength for those things that He has called us to do. Strength can also be interpreted ability in this passage of scripture. We see that the potential of man is on display through Paul's testimony of God's call.

In Romans 12:1-2 Paul writes, "I Beseech you therefore brethren, by the mercies of God that you (your human spirit) present your bodies a living sacrifice, holy and acceptable unto God, which is your reasonable service. And be not conformed to this world: but be ye transformed by the renewing of your mind, that ye may prove what is that good, and acceptable, and perfect will of God."

He tell us that we are too through our human spirit bring our body and mind under subjection to our spirit which is controlled by the Holy Spirit of God. Jesus cleansed our spirit but He left the renewing of the mind (soul of man) and the sacrifice of the body up to us. As we grow in the knowledge of God we increase in understanding of the principles of God as well as the character of God. The word of God indicates that God has created us with something called increase potential. Jesus said the reason God will prune us is so that we can produce more fruit. God always expects more from us than we are currently producing for him. The potential to be more for God rests inside of us.

Just as we are able to cause our physical bodies to increase in muscle mass through exercise and strength training we are also able to cause the five components of our soul to increase also. God has given this increase potential to us for our own growth. As we increase in the areas of our mind, will, imagination, emotions and our intellect we will begin to utilize the untapped ability that God has given each one of us. I am a firm believer in continuous growth and development in all areas of life. As we focus on the development of our soul we can witness this incredible principle at work. Let's examine each component starting with our mind. The mind has been referred to in the past as the first super computer on earth. It has the ability to retain, replicate, and reason. A sound mind is what we all want. It is in this area of our soul that makes us uniquely different from each other. The things that we allow to enter our minds play a significant part in our growth and development. As we learned earlier a seed is any thought you think, action you do and words you speak. The things we think, do and say are in direct per potion to what we have allowed to influence our thinking. Negative infiltration will often time result in negative actions. The opposite is also true. If we fill our minds with positive constructive information we will reap the benefits of the positive seeds we have sown. Your mind also has the ability to reason. This is one of many things that separate us from the other animal life on the planet. While animals live and respond to life out of basic instinct man kind responds out of his ability to reason. This ability to reason in its simplest form is the ability to determine what is right or wrong.

The greatest desire of mankind is to be in God's presence and to conform to the image of Jesus Christ. As we grow in the knowledge of God we are using our potential to become more like Jesus. At the point of salvation the spirit man has been redeemed and cleansed by the blood of Christ but the soul of man has not change. As a believer it is vitally important that we accept the presence and power of the Holy Spirit. It is the Holy Spirit of God that assists us with direction, instruction, correction and power to accomplish what God has called us to accomplish. When God gives us instruction he speaks to our spirit. God has given us a command that we should walk according to our Spirit and not after our flesh. When we surrender our spirit to the Holy Spirit of God and bring our soul and bodies into subjection to the Holy Spirit we will begin to recognize our purpose, passion and potential. It is the Holy Spirit that reminds us that we can do all things through Christ who strengthens us. It is the Holy Spirit that shows us what is to be accomplished through Him. It is the Holy Spirit that shows us the finished product of what God wants us to accomplish. It is the Holy Spirit that empowers us to attempt and accomplish the will of God.

The next area to be examined is the will. The will of man is also located in the soul. It is the component that serves as the object to be won in the war between Satan and the Holy Spirit. The battle is for the control of the will. It is from the will that man commands the body to carry out its decisions and desires. If Satan wins the battle for the will the body will execute the deeds of the flesh. However if the Holy Spirit wins the battle of the will we will experience the benefits of righteousness. Remember the battle being fought in the mind is for the will of man.

The imagination is the next area to be examined. The imagination is the third component of the soul or the mind. When the imagination is engaged we are able to see images of what the will of God looks like. These same images can be manipulated by Satan to entice us into unrighteousness. God created this component in the soul to accelerate the faith process. Whenever we hear words it creates images, and images create emotions and emotions create actions. God also uses the imagination to show you what is possible. The power of a visual image works as an internal motivator for God. As long as the images remain attached to the will of God we move towards accomplishing His will. This is the same tool that God used with Joshua when he was to take the city of Jericho. The book of Joshua chapter 6 verses 2 states, "And the Lord said unto Joshua, see, I have given into your hand Jericho, and the king thereof and the mighty men of valor." Notice that this statement came before Joshua had ever received the plan of action from God. The Lord instructed him to see on the canvass of his imagination himself and the children of Isreal victorious before they had ever fought the battle. One of my favorite sayings goes like this, "If you cannot see it before you see it, you will never see it." In other words if you can not picture it on the canvass of your own imagination you will never have the faith to cause it to materialize. God also gives us a bold command in scripture to combat the enemy when he attempts to pervert our thinking through our imagination. The word of God instructs us in 2 Corinthians 10:4-5 by stating, "For the weapons of our warfare are not carnal, but mighty through God to the pulling down of strongholds; casting down imaginations, and every high thing that exalts itself against the knowledge of God, and bringing into captivity every thought to the obedience of Christ." It is Gods intention that your very imagination be used for His glory and purpose only. The imagination component is so important to the development of your faith that God encourages us to stay connected to His word through out our entire lives. The tendency as we get older is to forsake our imaginations. We loose sight of what is possible, in other words we simply stop dreaming of greater. If we fail to stay connected to God we loose out on the possibilities that would be shown to us. The Holy Spirit, who knows the mind of God and is able to paint the correct picture when we stay connected to Him, will keep us focused on Gods will.

The fourth component of the soul or mind in the component called emotions. The emotions of man are so powerful that we allow them to move us into action on a consistent basis. However God never intended that this component be the determining factor for your behavior. Many live by their feelings and emotions and are thus tossed to and fro when their emotions change. The scripture teaches us that we are to live by every word that proceeds out of the mouth of God. When we do this we can rest assured that the emotions that create actions will be pleasing to God.

The fifth component is the component of intellect. Intellect is ones capacity for knowledge and reasoning. It is also the ability to come to correct conclusions. This component separates us from all of the other animal life forms on Earth. The word knowledge means "spiritual truth" or that which is "truth". In St. John 17:17 Jesus prays to the Father these words, "Sanctify them through thy truth, thy word is truth." He indicates in this passage of scripture that the only truth there is, is the Word of God. As we increase in spiritual truth (knowledge) we are expanding our intellectual capacity for more. The more spiritual truth you know and practice, the greater the assignment and responsibility God will entrust you with.

The Power to do More

The word potential comes from the root word potent which means power. The Holy Spirit is the expressed power of God in the earth and He lives in us. Therefore, we have all the power or potential we will ever need to accomplish His will. You may say, 'But I have never done that before." That's alright because that becomes your indicator of what potential you have inside of you. Based upon God's will for your life, what can you do but haven't done yet? What can you have but haven't obtained yet? What you can be but haven't become yet? All of these questions when answered give you a clear indication of the potential you possess.

Chapter 6

Kingdom Principle of Potential

Overview

Potential is your hidden strength and your untapped ability. It is what you can do but haven't done yet. It is what you can become but haven't become yet. It is what you can have but haven't obtained yet.

The Make Up of Mankind:

Your Spirit (The real you)

You're Soul (Five components of the soul are the mind, will, imagination, emotions and intellect.

You're Body (The physical house your spirit and soul lives in)

The greatest desire of mankind is to be in God's presence and to conform to the image of Jesus Christ.

The Power to do more

CHAPTER 7

The Kingdom Principle of Greatness

"But it shall not be so among you: but whosoever will be great among you, let him be your minister; and whosoever will be chief among you, let him be your servant...." St. Matthew 20:26-27

I was sitting in the sales manager's office when he asked me this question. He said, "How can we separate ourselves from our competition and become great?" I sat there eager to answer his question when the above scripture entered my mind. I began to speak of what it meant to be really great. It has been said in business that you can sell the same product as another and charge a greater price as long as the service you are providing with that product exceeds the customer's expectations. Until you can serve another at the level of their expectation you have not yet reached the highest level of greatness. The world has its own definition which is always contrary to the Word of God. The world says in order to be considered great you must have others who cater to your whims and desires. However, the Word of God says that to be great in the kingdom of God you must understand

and fully embrace what it means to be a servant. The fine art of serving seems to be a lost principle even among God's people. We must remember that we are only serving when the other person's expectations and needs have been met. The bible teaches that we are to not only have a mind to serve but a heart to serve. Jesus Christ the King of Glory said, "Even as the Son of man came not to be ministered unto, but to minister, and to give his life a ransom for many." St. Matthew 20:28

Jesus the Greatest Servant of All

Jesus demonstrates time and again His ability to serve at the highest level of His Fathers expectations. He knew that in doing so others would benefit and have their greatest need met. In the previous chapter I indicated that the greatest desire of mankind is to be in God's presence and to be conformed to the image of Jesus Christ. The sacrifice our Lord made on the cross at Calvary demonstrated His servant's heart and secured for us the opportunity to have our greatest desire fulfilled in Him. With his demonstration of obedience to serve His Father's will; Jesus set the example for everyone to follow.

To achieve greatness we must understand that we are here to do the will of God. Just as Jesus stated on many occasion that His only desire was to do the will of the Father who sent Him. The first thing that we must have is a **love** for the one we are called to serve and that is God. We must also have a love for those who will be recipients of our service. Second, we must have a clear **understanding** of what is expected from God our Father and the Lord Jesus Christ. Remember to act outside of the will of God serves Satan and not God. Third, we must be fully **committed** to God the one who we have been called to serve as well as the ones who will be the beneficiary of our service. Fourth, we must **obey** the will of God completely just as Jesus did.

A Need to Serve

True greatness is energized by the love and desire to see others benefit. Inside of every person is the desire to be great however, if we are not connected to God through His son Jesus you will not know that the will of God is to serve Him and others and not to seek to serve ones self. I have often said that the opposite of love is not hate but selfishness. When we seek our own will and not the will of God only we ultimately bring about hurt and pain to ourselves and to others. God's original plan for all of mankind was to always do His will. His perfect will always bring about the absolute best for us.

True greatness also requires sacrifice. Sacrifice is giving even when it requires going above and beyond your initial expectations. Serving in its purest form is giving and giving is an attribute of love. The Word of God teaches us that God is love. It does not say that God possesses love but that He is love. The expression of love is demonstrated through giving. We know that everything created and made was created and made to benefit something outside of itself. Even the fulfilling of purpose is manifested through giving. Greatness is always the end result when we give what and how God has required us to give. The will of God is that we demonstrate our greatness and His love by serving others with our time, talents, gifts, abilities and our treasure. God's ultimate expression of

His greatness and love is found in St. John 3:16-17. It says, "For God so loved the world, that he gave his only begotten Son, that whosoever believeth in him should not perish but have everlasting life. For God sent not his Son into the world to condemn the world; but that the world through him might be saved." Jesus later said in the same book of John chapter 15 in verse 13 these words, "Greater love hath no man than this that a man lay down his life for his friends." Here the Lord speaks of and later demonstrates His greatness in sacrifice, obedience, love and commitment to His Fathers will. What an awesome God we serve!

A Mind to Serve

We as the elect children of God not only have a need to serve but the mind to serve. In the book of Romans chapter 12 verse 2 Paul writes, "And be not conformed to this world; but be ye transformed by the renewing of your mind, that you may prove what is that good, and acceptable, and perfect will of God." He reminds us that once we are converted that we have to change the way we think. When we were in the world we thought as the world thinks. We know that in the world there is a selfishness that consumes the mind of those who walk in darkness. However once we come to the knowledge of Jesus we are to take on his mind. In the book of Philippians 2:2-5 Paul writes, "Fulfill ye my joy, that ye be likeminded, having the same love, being of one accord, of one mind. Let nothing be done through strife (self seeking will) or vain glory; but in lowliness of mind let each esteem other better than themselves. Look not every man on his own things, but every man also on the things of others. Let this mind be in you, which was also in Christ Jesus." The mind of Jesus was to always do the will of the Father and to serve others with love and compassion. Is this mind in you?

A Heart to Serve

I have come to know that we only respond to life out of our own belief system. Whatever is in the heart will appear in your life. In other words what a person says and does is a direct product of what is in their heart. Proverbs 4:23 says, "Keep your heart with all diligence; for out of it are the issues of life." You can always tell what is in a person's heart by simply watching what they do. Many times we hear people say that no one knows my heart but God. Ultimately that is a relatively true statement however, people may not know the motives that drive your decisions (only God know that) but what they do know is what is in your heart by what is appearing in your life through your choices. The scripture says, "For the word of God is quick, and powerful and sharper than any two edged sword, piercing even to the dividing asunder of soul and spirit, and of the joints and marrow, and is a discerner of the thoughts and intents of the heart." (Hebrews 4:12) The intent is the reason or motive of why you do what you do. We as believers are to have the heart to be great and a heart to serve God through serving others. If the Spirit of God dwells in you then you also have the heart to serve. It may not be clear to you at this time where and in what capacity you are to be serving but God through the Holy Spirit in prayer will reveal that to you.

A Commitment to Serve

I was listening to a friend speak in an effort to evangelize a non believer in Christ. As she spoke she made the comment to the person that they should try Jesus because they have tried everything else. In her innocence she failed to communicate that you don't try Jesus as if He is a practice and not the ultimate principle, you commit to Jesus as Lord and King. I began to think how many others are simply trying Jesus and not fully committing to Him? When we commit to Jesus our will no longer exists and we take on the will of him who called us. Commitment is also an expression of love. Jesus committed to the will of the Father unto the very end of his earthly assignment. Because we were created for His purpose we must also commit to Jesus until our earthly assignment is complete. Everyday through prayer we must search out the will of God for that day. When we do this the Holy Spirit will direct our path and lead us into our assignment of serving for that day. There is nothing more fulfilling to mankind and nothing more pleasing to God than to do the will of Him who called us. Remember you don't try Jesus you simply commit to Him.

Ask yourself a question are you fully committed to God or are you just trying Him? There is an old wise proverb that states you cannot swim with one foot on the bank. If you are fully engaged in God's purpose for your life continue on the path the Holy Spirit is leading you on. If you cannot answer the question with a resounding yes let us stop now and pray the prayer of repentance and rededicate yourself to the will of God. Say these words with me. "Father, I come to you as your servant and child. I repent for my lack of commitment to your will for my life. I ask that you forgive me and set me back on the path of righteousness. Father I rededicate myself to you now. Help me to keep my commitment to you. Father, thank you for forgiving me and I receive your forgiveness right now in Jesus name. Amen."

Chapter 7

"The Kingdom Principle of Greatness"

Overview

Jesus the greatest servant of all was our model. He lived out the Fathers purpose and exceeded the expectations of those he served.

A need to serve is an evident desire inside of us all to give our best for the betterment of others. "Everything in life was created and made to benefit something outside of itself."

A mind to serve must be cultivated in us. It is God's intention to develop in us the mind of Christ. To have a mind fixed on doing the will of God.

A heart to serve, this must be our ultimate state of being. The scripture teaches that out of our heart flows the issues of life. Our entire life must be a demonstration of our heart to serve. As Jesus demonstrated daily, we must also demonstrate daily our heart to serve.

A commitment to serve has to become our way of life. We know that nothing is done in excellence until a commitment is made. Serving at the highest level of God's expectation takes an unwavering commitment to live for Christ. As I have said many times, "you don't try God you commit to Him."

CHAPTER 8

The Kingdom Principle of Forgiveness

"But if you do not forgive, neither will your Father which is in heaven forgive your trespasses." St. Mark 11:26

I have been very fortunate and blessed in my life in all aspects but there is one area I feel I have been particularly blessed in. That area is the area of forgiveness. From a child I have always had a heart for those who are hurting. I was aware at a young age that when a person is hurt they usually hurt others. This is where the Cranism of "hurting people hurt people" comes from. While sitting in the hallway window looking down on the argument that had started, I noticed that one of the young girls whose sister was one of the soon to be combatants had picked up a broken bottle by the neck and held it to her side. As the other girl and her sister continued to argue and curse at each other the hurling words soon turned to hurling fists. When the crowd gathered to watch I kept my eyes fixed on the girl with the broken bottle. After a short while the girls were fully entangled in an all out fight. As soon as the girl's sister had gotten an advantage over the other smaller girl, the girl with the broken bottle reached in and cut the face of the smaller girl who was being held by her sister. As blood began to flow from her face the older larger girl released her and the fight was broken up by neighboring adults. The younger girl who had done the damage yelled out to the girl who was cut and said, "I will never forgive you for what you said about my sister." Later on that day I found out that the smaller girl had made reference to the larger girl's size calling her fat. This is what set off the hideous violence that ensued. Later that night, I began to reflect on what had taken place. I replayed the events in my head and wondered what level of hurt was inside the heart of the young girl to make her lash out in such a violent way. As my heart went out to the young girl who had been cut I found myself feeling more sorry for the girl who had done the cutting. All I could think about was how and when she would be freed from the hurt that was driving her words and actions. It was crystal clear to me she needed not only to be forgiven for her actions but she needed to forgive those who had caused her hurt in the past. She needed the comfort and knowledge of the Saviors love for forgiveness to really be set free.

The damage caused by an unforgiving heart

Whenever we are hurt spiritually or emotionally we must choose the correct response. The old saying that states what you don't know won't hurt you does not apply in the Kingdom of God. What you don't know and don't understand will lead to misery, poverty, sickness and ultimately death both physically and spiritually. When we don't fully understand the principle of forgiveness it is possible to activate this principle against yourself and thus cause a string of events that will keep you trapped in that ultimate state of pain and confusion until you accept God's plan of redemption. When we are hurt we are forced to make a decision on how we are going to mange the pain we are feeling. Jesus tells us that we are to forgive those who have hurt us and to pray for those who despitefully misuse us. However, many believers are in the revenge business and have no intentions of forgiving anyone who has ever wronged them. In the scriptures God teaches us that the heart of man is the soil in which the seeds of life are planted. If the heart is not free from hurt and pain, malice and strife, bitterness and un forgiveness we will not be able to produce those things that are pleasing to God. The scripture teaches that God is Love and the manifestation of all that God does is always in love. 1 Timothy 1:5 makes this very truth clear by stating; "Now the end (purpose) of the commandment is charity (love) out of a pure heart, and a good conscience, and of faith unfeigned." Forgiveness is a Kingdom principle of God that exhibits His love and must be adhered to in order to please Him. We know that whatever is appearing in our life is a product of what is in our heart.

Only two choices

One of my favorite sayings is this, "You will either live your life by the principles of the word or by the practices of the world." The book of Proverbs chapter 3:5-6 states, "Trust in the Lord with all thine heart; and lean not to thy own understanding. In all thy ways acknowledge Him and he shall direct thy paths." Just like every situation we face in life we have a choice to do things God's way or to lean to our own understanding. This scripture tells us how we are to handle every situation we are faced with.

It simply tells us that we are to acknowledge God. We are to find out from God how we are to manage every situation we face. This includes our hurts and pains. The choices we make already have the consequences built into them. As a young man I was not aware of how to make the right choices in life. I often thought that you simply did what you wanted and let the chips fall where they may. Needless to say I have had many days of heart ache and pain. The correct way is in the knowledge of Proverbs 15:1. The Word of God say's, "A soft answer turns away wrath: but grievous words stir up anger." The scripture teaches us about the power of choice. It indicates that every choice has a consequence already attached to it. It says that if I choose a soft answer the consequence will be that wrath will be turned away. However, if I choose grievous words it will stir up anger. You cannot choose one without the other. The choice and consequence are opposite sides of the same coin. Once we come to understand this principle of choice we will choose based on the consequences we want to have in life and not just the immediate pleasure no matter how tempting it may appear to be. Here we see that if we choose to trust in the Lord and acknowledge him the consequence will be that He will direct our paths. However if we lean to our own understanding he will not direct our path and we are left to navigate through the confusion and difficulty we will face. I have yet to meet the person who can effectively manage the pain and confusion that comes along with a heart of un forgiveness. It all begins with a choice to acknowledge Him. In doing so, He will direct us down the path of forgiveness and healing.

God has consistently tried through His Word and His Spirit to get us his children to live by revelation and not sensation. To live by revelation is to live by the revealed truth of His Word. To live by sensation is to live by your feelings. This is completely against the will of God. How we feel about a situation should never determine how or what we should do. We should only live life based on the truth of God's word. Whenever we choose to respond to life's challenges based on our feelings and not God's word we open ourselves up to fall and to be led astray from the path God has laid out for us. I stated earlier that one of the things the believer will experience is poverty when they stray away from the path. The reason they experience lack when they stray away is because the blessings of God are positional. Think of it this way. If you were to go on a long journey and planned your trip effectively you would set up strategic points along the way. Those strategic points would have the necessary provisions you needed to get you to your next strategic point. This is exactly what God has done for you in this life. Your blessings and provisions are already strategically placed. As you obey the instructions of the Holy Spirit he directs you and leads you into God's divine purpose. This is a part of what Jesus meant when he said the Holy Spirit will lead you and guide you into all truth and righteousness (St John 16:13).

The choices are simple. They are, "Trust in the Lord with all your heart and to lean not to your own understanding, and to acknowledge Him in all your ways and he will direct your paths."

As I stated earlier I have yet to meet the person who can effectively manage their emotional state without the presence of God and the direction of the Holy Spirit. Jesus said in St. John 15:5,"….. for without me you can do nothing." Whenever we choose not to forgive we are leaning to our own understanding. Whenever we choose not to forgive we are not acknowledging Him. We simply have made the wrong choices. Not choosing God's way means that we will not be able to manage our emotional state. Not being able to manage your emotional state leads to (4) devastating outcomes. They are perpetual sin, addictions, bitterness and un forgiveness. Let's take a look at each one separately and the devastation it causes.

Perpetual Sin

Perpetual sin is a repeated act of disobedience that appears to be uncontrollable. How many times have you asked God to forgive you for the same sin? You promise God and yourself that you would no longer engage in that sin but you find yourself drawn to it only to participate in it again. This perpetual sin leads you to doubt your own commitment to God and God's commitment to you. It distorts our right thinking because we have strayed away from the path of God. This is the first thing that happens when we mismanage our emotional state. Hebrews 12:1 states, ".....let us lay aside every weight, and the sin which does so easily best us ...." The medication for emotional and spiritual hurt is not perpetual sin but the blood of Jesus.

Addictions

I define addiction as any compulsive, unrighteous behavior used as a consistent substitute for mismanaged emotions. It is the highest form of idolatry. I was flipping through the channels one night and came across a television program called "Strange Addictions." I had never seen it before but this particular program featured two women. One was addicted to eating rocks and the other one was addicted to carrying a pillow everywhere she went. It was strange to see their addictions play out in such an uncommon way. When we think of addiction we often think only in terms of alcohol, food, and drug use as the most obvious. During one of the narrative excerpts the speaker made the comment that the young lady who carried the pillow was at one point exploited and sexually abused at a young age. She said, "After the trauma of being abused I simply clung to my pillow for comfort and support." She also made the statement, "My pillow listens to me and does not judge me." These are common statements that indicate that the hurt that was inflicted has not been dealt with correctly and therefore her emotional state is being mismanaged. This is a common response for all who suffer from addictions. Even the woman who was addicted to eating rocks found a form of false security and comfort in an unnatural behavior. The common theme with all people who are addicted is there is a reference point that can be traced back to a moment where they were physically, emotionally or spiritually hurt and did not choose the correct response to deal with the hurt. With all mismanaged emotions the remedy is the same it is applying the kingdom principle of forgiveness and the shed blood of Jesus to the wounded area.

Bitterness

Hebrews 12:15 says, "Looking diligently lest any man fail of the grace of God; lest any root of bitterness springing up trouble you, and there by many be defiled." This passage of scripture indicates that bitterness is seen as a seed and therefore has a root. If the emotional state is mismanaged this root of bitterness will spring up and cause you trouble. The seed of bitterness in you will also cause others to be defiled. As I wrote in a previous chapter that challenges in life can come by human error. These are mistakes caused by others. The Word of God says that this is indeed possible if we mismanage our emotional state. Bitterness not only affects you but others around you who are also connected to your life.

Unforgiveness is the end game

I am a firm believer that many Christians fail to recognize the significance of the kingdom principle of forgiveness. Many believe that it is possible to have a complete relationship with God and have malice or hatred in their heart for others. They also believe that God is somehow endorsing this behavior. I believe that once you have been forgiven of your sins and understand the magnitude of what that really means you will be forgiving of others for their sins. The scripture says, "For all have sinned and come short of the glory of God." (Romans 3:23) Jesus the King of Glory hung on a cross and shed his blood for the remission of our sins. He alone paid our sin debt so that we can enjoy the presence and Kingdom of God once more. His death on the cross gave back to us the right to come before the throne of grace as children of the highest God. To get a true revelation of this just reflect back on the things that God has forgiven you for.

The reason that forgiveness is so important is found in the book of St. Mark chapter 11 verses 25-26. It states, "And when you stand praying forgive, if you have aught against anyone: that your Father also which is in heaven may forgive you your trespasses. But if you do not forgive, neither will your Father which is in heaven forgive your trespasses." This passage is so important because it tells us that by holding un forgiveness in our hearts we cancel the salvation on our life that was freely given to us. Satan knows if he can get the believer to harbor un forgiveness in their heart they will forfeit their salvation and spend eternity in hell with him. This is his game plan for mankind. The word says that if we fail to forgive others God will not forgive us and if God does not forgive us our sins then salvation can not be granted. Many believers are oblivious to this kingdom principle.

My encouragement to you is to manage your emotional state by applying the kingdom principle of forgiveness. We all are faced with unpleasant and hurting situations in our lives however, we have an advocate in Jesus and the power of the Holy Spirit to see us through it. One of my favorite verses is found in Psalms 34:19 it states, "Many are the afflictions of the righteous: but the Lord delivers him out of them all." That's an incredible promise from our Father.

A final thought about forgiveness

It has been said that, "Holding un forgiveness in your heart is like you drinking poison and hoping someone else dies." The un forgiveness in your heart only hurts you. When you don't forgive you allow others and Satan to have a place in your life that was only reserved for God. That is the place of authority. Satan should never be allowed to dictate your behavior. As children of God we are lead by the Spirit of God only.

The Lord reminded me to tell his children that the spirit of apathy is not a substitute for forgiveness. This simply means that saying I don't care anymore (the spirit of apathy) is not acceptable as a substitute for forgiving others.

A prayer for forgiveness

Heavenly Father I come to you today with a heart that has been hurt. I know that I have harbored un forgiveness in my heart against others and I now recognize that I can go no further in life without your forgiveness. Father at this very moment I repent of my sins and release those who have hurt me in the past. Father I forgive them. I no longer hold any malice in my heart toward them for anything that was ever done. Wash me now with the blood of Jesus and cleanse me from a heart of un forgiveness. Father you said in your Word that if I confess my sins you are faithful and just to forgive my sins and to cleanse me from all unrighteousness. Father, I thank you. Thank you for giving me the courage and strength to forgive others. I know this is the will of God for my life. In Jesus name I ask and receive your forgiveness Amen.

Chapter 8

"The Kingdom Principle of Forgiveness"

Overview

Damage caused by an un forgiving heart- We must choose the correct response when we are hurt spiritually and emotionally. Not choosing the correct response leads to misery, poverty, sickness and death both spiritually and physically.

Only two choices- Proverbs 3:5-6 states, "Trust in the Lord with all thine heart; and lean not to your own understanding. In all your ways acknowledge him and he shall direct your paths." We will either trust in the Lord or we will lean to our own understanding. There are only two choices.

Mismanaged emotions lead to:

- Perpetual sin
- Addictions
- Bitterness
- Un forgiveness

Final thought about un forgiveness- "Un forgiveness in your heart is like you drinking poison and hoping someone else will die" Un forgiveness in your heart only hurts you.

A prayer for forgiveness

CHAPTER 9

The Kingdom Principle of Unity

"Behold how good and how pleasant it for bretheren to dwell together in unity" Psalms 133:1

When I was a young man starting out on my faith journey I like many others had a lot of questions. I remember a specific conversation I had with my mentor. I asked him, "Why were there so many different churches and why didn't every one attend the same church?" This I asked because for as long as I could remember most of the churches in my neighborhood were never filled and I couldn't remember them ever making a profound impact on our community. He answered me by explaining the scriptures that are found in the book of Ephesians chapter 4 beginning with verse 11-16. It reads, "And he gave some, apostles; and some prophets; and some evangelists; and some, pastors and teachers; (v:12) For the perfecting (maturing) of the saints, for the work of the ministry, for the edifying of the body of Christ: (v:13) Till we all come in the unity of the faith, and of the knowledge of the Son of God, unto a perfect man, unto the measure of the stature of the fullness of Christ: (v:14) That we henceforth be no more children, tossed to and fro, and carried about with every wind of doctrine, by the sleight of men, and cunning craftiness, whereby they lie in wait to deceive; (v:15)But speaking the truth in love, may grow up into him in all things, which is the head, even Christ: (v:16) From whom the whole body fitly joined together and compacted by that which every joint supplies, according to the effectual working in the measure of every part, makes increase of the body unto the edifying of itself in love." He made specific reference to verse thirteen and the coming into the unity of the faith and the knowledge of the Son of God, unto a perfect man and unto the measure of the stature of the fullness of Christ. He explained what this meant by sharing with me this experience. Every year in my community we host a fair. Just like many other community fairs this one offered many games, rides and attractions. It was one of these attractions that caught his attention. As he walked he noticed a sign that read come see the world's smallest man. Being intrigued by the sign and the pitch from the Carney man he decided to pay his money and go inside. Looking inside he could only see a small fence that stood about four feet high. When it was his turn to view what was on the other side of the fence he hesitated and asked the Carney man who was standing there, "Is there really a person behind that small fence?" The Carney man replied, "It's your turn step up and take a look." Walking to the fence and looking over he saw an actual man standing there. The man had the body of a child but the head of a fully grown man. The man met his gaze with a smile and a wave. Being satisfied with what he had seen he turned and walked away. He then stated to me that the Spirit of God had said, "This is what the church looks like." The head which is Christ is fully grown; however the body is still maturing and developing to measure up to the fullness of the stature of Christ. The five fold ministries were given as gifts from Christ to assist the members of the body in its quest to mature and unify. The unfortunate part was realizing that the only way that could happen was through a unified effort of seeing Christ as our head and the need to grow and measure up to Him and not one another. Just like most of the neighborhood and most of society we have been disappointed realizing that becoming unified was a principle that was much easier said than done.

The Power of Unity

For anyone who has ever worked on a particular task with others and has come across those who were willing to work together for one common goal, you have a taste of the power of unity. The founding fathers of this great country understood the concept of unity best. They knew that as long as they were unified they could not only stand up to the tyranny of the British but could also establish themselves as a future country. It was their understanding of unity that prompted them to establish their colonies under one banner that we so proudly call the United States of America. I am a firm believer that any group of people who are unified has the power in itself to accomplish its goals and purpose. The book of Genesis 11:5-6 says, "And the Lord came down to see the city and the tower, which the children of men builded. And the Lord said, Behold, the people is one, and they have all one language; and this they begin to do: and now nothing will be restrained from them which they imagine to do." The scripture indicates that because the people were all unified in their words, actions and intentions that nothing would be restrained from them that they have imagined. The power to accomplish a task is found in the principle of unity.

A Commanded Blessing

The foundational scripture for this chapter on unity began with Psalms 133 and verse one. However to get the full meaning and understanding of the principle we must read all three verses of the chapter. It says, "Behold how good and how pleasant it is for breathern to dwell together in unity! It is like the precious ointment upon the head that ran down upon the beard even Aaron's beard: that went down to the skirts of his garments; as the dew of Hermon, and as the dew that descended upon the mountains of Zion: for there the Lord commanded the blessings, even life for evermore." Verse three tells us that the Lord commanded the blessings, even life evermore at the point of unity. The oil that was poured on the head of Aaron the high priest of Isreal signified the anointing of God and his very presence. As the oil flowed in one direction and came together in one place at the hem of his garments the blessings of the Lord were commanded there. At the point of the oil coming together, better expressed as the point of unity, the Lord commanded his blessings forever more. The commanded blessings of the Lord have been established by God and are released through the unified efforts of the children of God.

Unified With the Father, the Son and the Holy Spirit

The entire creation of God works consistent with the kingdom principle of unity. It is inside of this principle that we share in the kingdom promises that our Lord and Savior Jesus Christ merited for us on the cross. Through his finished work we can once again be united with the Father, the Son and the Holy Spirit. It should not only be our greatest joy but our only one. Throughout scripture Jesus would often make reference to him and the Father being one. The Lord being our example on Earth demonstrated that being one with the Father was his greatest joy. He was able to accomplish this even in his earthly form by submitting to the will of the Father in all things. One of the things Jesus merited for us through his finished works was the opportunity to be unified once again with the Father. It has always been God's purpose for us to be unified with Him through his son Jesus. God has given us his Son as the necessary sacrifice to atone for our sins. He has also given us free access to himself through Jesus. He has given us freely the gift of his Holy Spirit to be with us at all times. This alone demonstrates how important being unified with him really is. In doing so he has given us the ability to be of one mind, one Spirit, one understanding and one purpose with him. All of God's children have this same promise of unity with the Father, the Son and the Holy Spirit. Isn't it a wonderful thing to know that The Father, the Son and the Holy Spirit desire for us to be reunited with them as one? As a believer we must also come to embrace the knowledge of who He is and His will for our lives. God not only intends for us to be reunited with Him but to also be united with one another to accomplish His will in the Earth. It is through unity that the will of God is made evident in the lives of all mankind. This is His original and everlasting plan for us. To all be of one mind, one Spirit, one understanding and one purpose of heart is what it really means to be unified with the Father, the Son and the Holy Spirit.

Only Unity gets rid of the big demons

For many years our congregation was very small. It has since grown. However I remember thinking often why the ministry experienced what I would consider a high rate of turn over. There would be many people who would come in for awhile and then depart. There was no real follow up system in place to track why they were not staying so there is no real data to accurately determine the reason(s) for sure. I know this was a concern for the Pastor as well as some of the core members who had been there for a while. We were all speechless at times when we would here that members would just stop coming with no real explanation. On one Sunday morning the Pastor spoke to the congregation concerning this issue. He said that he took the matter before the Lord and was given a vision from God that explained why this was happening so frequently. He stated that the Lord showed him our church building, which was a large former Catholic church that was much larger than our congregation could support at the time, and a very large demon spirit standing next to it. As he looked on in amazement he stated that the demon then stretched his body over the entire church building blanketing it on all sides until it was completely covered. He said at that point the Lord spoke to him and said, "The demon is the spirit of apathy." The spirit of apathy is a spirit that causes a believer to think and say, "I don't care anymore." This demon spirit is both a serious and subtle demon. Many believers are falling prey to this same I don't care spirit of apathy. The serious part is that this spirit wrecks any attempts at progress and fulfilling the will of God. The subtle part is many are experiencing this not only in their ministries but also in their personal lives as well. For employers they are trying to understand why their employees are not performing up to expectations, for families' parents are wondering why their children have this I don't care attitude. The reason this demon spirit is allowed to operate is because of a lack of unity. After the Pastor shared what the Lord said to him he also stated that the Lord said, "It takes unity to get rid of the big demons." There it was the answer to our dilemma. We were not all unified in our words or actions. We were not all of one mind, one Spirit, one understanding and one purpose. Therefore, we were not benefiting from the kingdom principle of unity.

Take a moment and reflect on your personal life. Are you being victimized by the demon spirit of apathy, that I don't care attitude in your career, your relationship with family members and friends or possibly your spouse? If so remember it has always been God's will that we are unified in our efforts when it comes to our relationship with Him and others. The answer is simple; it takes unity to get rid of the big demons.

A Prayer for you

Heavenly Father, I come to you now recognizing your principle of unity and power. I ask that you bind us as believers together with cords of love. Give us one mind and one understanding. As you, your son Jesus and the Holy Spirit are one continue to make us one in you. Father, as I practice this principle I live in expectation of experiencing your commanded blessings just as you have promised. I receive them now by faith in the name of Jesus Christ my King. Amen.

Chapter 9

The Kingdom Principle of Unity

Overview

The power of unity- There is a unique power associated with having the same mind, purpose, speech and action.

A commanded blessing- The Word of God teaches us that at the point of unity God commands His blessings forever more.

Unified with the Father, the Son and the Holy Spirit- It has always been God's intention that mankind stay connected to Him at all times. After the fall of man Jesus made that possible again.

Only unity gets rid of the big demons- You may be facing the spirit of apathy in your home, workplace or your personal life. If so, remember only unity gets rid of the big demons.

CHAPTER 10

The Kingdom Principle of Agreement

"Again I say unto you, that if two of you shall agree on earth as touching any thing that they shall ask, it shall be done for them of my Father which is in heaven. For where two or three are gathered together in my name, there am I in the midst of them." St. Matthew 18:19-20

I have witnessed over the years the harsh reality of verbal conflict. It is often driven by a selfish attitude or behavior. However, the goal and end result of every argument must be to reach an agreement. To state or express an opinion is a part of growth and development but to vehemently argue a point with another is the result of different belief systems. When this revelation of truth was revealed to me it was directly after witnessing a respected married couple in a physical altercation. I have no idea to this day what started the fight but I do remember thinking, why was this happening and why they just simply couldn't agree? The answer was they had different beliefs about the matter. Not just a difference of opinion but different beliefs. I realized that this respected couple had no real idea that marriage was an agreement between the husband and the wife but a covenant with God.

The Power of Agreement

In our foundational scripture of Matthew 18:19-20 we see that Jesus tells us of the power of agreement. Many who do not understand the principle may think that it is too fantastic to believe. Jesus states, "…that if two of you shall agree on earth as touching any thing that they shall ask, it shall be done for them of my Father which is in heaven." He indicates that the Father will do for you what you and at least one other on earth can agree on. We know that it has to be according to his will. Jesus being our example said that he always did the will of the Father who sent him. This kingdom principle gives incredible power to those who are married. The unfortunate part is many married couples find out the power of the principle after having gone through tremendous pains. Just think how rewarding a marriage can be if the Father was responsible for providing everything you wanted and desired. It has all been made available to you through the kingdom principle of agreement. Those who are married and find themselves living a silent divorce, that is to say that they are going through the motions with no real intent or desire to see the relationship grow, have not been made aware of this principle or simple don't understand its power. God's intent for marriage was to provide companionship for the man and woman so that their needs would be met inside the confines of His established covenant. Just think you have a spouse who has the capability to meet your needs and you have the ability to meet theirs. However, neither one is interested in practicing this kingdom principle in order to get their needs met. According to the Word of God when two people gets married God no longer considers them as two separate individuals but one unit. When two people are unified they have the same mind, the same speech, the same heart and therefore have the same actions. God says that when this principle is activated by touching and agreeing about anything on earth He will do it for you. Wow! How can you lose? I have found that the climate for any relationship can and will change with the activation of this kingdom principle. When a husband and wife are in agreement they not only get the benefits of what they are agreeing on but they get to experience what it really means to be in covenant with God. He promised in his word that if two agree on earth concerning anything the Father will do it for them. With out understanding this kingdom principle husbands and wives are left in a lifeless unfulfilled marriage and always on the verge of breaking their agreement with each other and breaking their covenant with God through divorce.

I was on my way to the church when I heard the Lord speak to me to call a particular brother in the church. As I picked up the phone and dialed his number I was again impressed in my heart to share this principle with him. As I began to speak he acknowledged that he and his wife were going through their most challenging time in their 8 year marriage. He mentioned to me that he had lost all desire to continue in the relationship and didn't know what was happening to him. As we talked he mentioned that his job would keep him away from home and on the road for extended periods of time. He noticed that the longer he was away the harder it was to reconnect with his wife no matter how hard she tried. I shared the foundational scripture with him and asked if there was anything that he and his wife could agree on? I told him it didn't have to be anything major but to make sure that it was something they could both agree on. And during the process of asking make sure that he held her hand as he was doing it. I explained the kingdom principle to him and asked him to trust the word of God for the results. We spoke at length about him regaining his desire for the marriage through touching and agreeing with his wife for their union. I have been observing their behavior over the past few weeks and have noticed a change in their behavior toward each other. There seems to be a renewed fire between them. I can't speak at length about their on going commitment to one another but I can testify to the fact that they are experiencing a greater love and understanding after having activating the kingdom principle of agreement.

Salvation the Ultimate State of Agreement

My heart goes out to every person who has heard the gospel of Jesus Christ and rejected it. It saddens me to see those who profess to be a witness of God but denies the entrance into God's holy presence. Jesus makes one of the most powerful declarations of who He is in the gospel of John chapter 14 verses 6. He states, "I am the way, the truth, and the life: no man comes to the Father, but by me." Even with this clear explanation of how to get back to our original place of being in God's holy presence many still reject the truth and forfeit their right to the kingdom of God through salvation. Jesus experienced the same heart felt sadness and spoke consistently to those who rejected Him as the Savior of the world. In the gospel of Matthew 23:13 Jesus makes this statement to the scribes and Pharisees, "But woe unto you, scribes and Pharisees, hypocrites! For you shut up the kingdom of heaven against men: for you neither go in yourselves, neither do you allow them that are entering to go in." Let us therefore be mindful of our action and not put a stumbling block in our brother's way but help them find their way to Jesus as we have.

Salvation takes place when there is true repentance for the sins we have committed and the acceptance of Jesus Christ as our Lord and Savior. Romans 10:9 states, "That if thou shall confess with thy mouth the Lord Jesus and shall believe in your heart that God has raised him from the dead, you shall be saved. True repentance is simply agreeing with God and turning away from everything that is contrary to His holy word. This free gift alone makes salvation the ultimate state of agreement. The principle states that if we agree here on earth concerning anything that is His will it shall be done for us by Him. The single most important agreement that we can make is when we agree that we need a savior and recognize that God has provided for us both a redeemer and a savior, his only begotten son, Jesus. What an incredible God we serve!

Agreement based on Truth and not Popularity

The understanding of the scripture which states that we are in the world but not of the world has never been more evident than living in a democratic society. This statement is not meant to belittle the benefits we are afforded by living in the greatest country on earth. It is however meant to make us aware that as believers we live in this world but we are not to confuse the world s system with the principles of the kingdom of God. Popularity is not a kingdom principle of God. The world's system of government is based in popularity and not necessarily the truth of God's word. All of the principles of the kingdom of God are founded on truth and love. In St. John 17:17 Jesus says, "Sanctify them through thy truth: thy word is truth." In this declaration Jesus tells us that the only truth there is are the words of God. Many of the worlds problems exist because we attempt to govern our lives by what is most popular that is to say the world's system and not by the truth of the word of God. Every believer must resist the temptation to do what is most popular when it is against the truth of God's word.

Jesus said if you love me you will keep my commandments. To keep the commandments of the Lord and to do his will means that we have to be in total agreement with the word of God. To agree with the word of God may not always be what is most popular but it will always be what is right. Agreement based on the truth of God's word and not popularity will assure us of always having God's best.

Divide and Conquer the Weapon of the Enemy

We spoke earlier about the importance of every married couple and believer understanding the kingdom principle of agreement. Without this understanding and application you assure yourself of not having God's best and open up an avenue for Satan to gain an advantage. One of the greatest military strategies has always been the strategy of divide and conquers.

Whenever we are ignorant of a kingdom principle we open ourselves up to the possibility of having that kingdom principle worked against us. Hosea 4:6a says, "My people are destroyed for lack of knowledge…" The word destroyed here means to render useless forever. The word knowledge refers to spiritual truth. In other words it means the people of God are rendered useless forever because of a lack of understanding concerning spiritual truth. Since the beginning in the Garden of Eden, Satan has used this tactic to take advantage of the children of God. His strategy is to cause division by questioning the validity of the Word of God. Whenever he can get us to disagree with the truth he has the opening he needs to come in and attempt a take over. Just like Adam when he agreed with Satan through sin and lost the kingdom of God and all that it represented, we are subject to lose all that we have when we agree with Satan through sin also. We must all come to the knowledge that says we are either agreeing with God through our actions and words or we are agreeing with Satan through our actions and words. There are no other choices. Divide and conquer in marriage is to get one of the spouses to agree with Satan directly or subtly. Either way it gives him the opening he needs to wreak havoc in that area of the marriage. Remember Satan only has jurisdiction in the darkness. Whenever we are walking in truth; the light form the truth and the power of the word holds the enemy at bay. The strategy of divide and conquer can only be effective when we are willing to entertain living a life outside of the word of God.

True Repentance is agreeing with the Word

Turing away from ungodliness and agreeing with the Word of God is true repentance. With true repentance we gain access to God the Father through Jesus Christ and the Holy Spirit. The Holy Scriptures in 1 John 5:6-12 says it best. It states, "This is he that came by water and blood, even Jesus Christ; not by water only but by water and blood. And it is the Spirit that bears witness, because the Spirit is truth. For there are three that bear record in heaven, the Father, the Word, and the Holy Ghost: and these three are one. And there are three that bear witness in earth, the spirit, and the water, and the blood: and these three agree in one. If we receive the witness of men, the witness of God is greater: for this is the witness of God which he has testified of his Son. He that believes on the Son of God has the witness in himself: he that believes not God has made him a liar; because he believes not the record that God gave of his Son. And this is the record that God has given to us eternal life, and this life is in his Son. He that has the Son has life; and he that has not the Son of God has not life."

"I call heaven and earth to record this day against you, that I have set before you life and death, blessings and cursing: therefore choose life that you and your seed may live." Deuteronomy 30:19

The Process of True Repentance

Ask most believers what does it mean to repent and you will probably get several different responses. Many will say it means to turn from our wicked ways. I contend that that is a part of the repentance process but it does not cover the totality of the process. The principle of repentance was so important to God that it became the first declaration of Jesus earthly ministry. He said, "Repent: for the kingdom of heaven is at hand." (Ref. St. Matthew 4:17) Here we see that repentance is the first thing that is required to gain access to the kingdom. The kingdom principle of repentance and its process are found in 2 Chronicles 7:14. It states, "If my people, which are called by my name, shall humble themselves, and pray, and seek my face, and turn from their wicked ways; then will I hear from heaven, and will forgive their sin, and will heal their land." Notice, that there are (4) specific things a person must do to truly repent according to the Word of God. The first thing that must be done is to humble ourselves. To become humble simply means to become teachable. It means, to realize that the wisdom you possess is not sufficient to accomplish what God has intended. The second thing that must be done is to pray. Prayer as we know is getting God involved in the situation. Remember, God has given dominion of this earth to man and will not intervene unless he is invited into the situation through prayer. Prayer is how we communicate with God. The third component of repentance is to seek the face of God. It is ironic that after Adams sin he and his wife chose to hide themselves from the face of God. This has been an ongoing practice among many believers today. Once a sinful act has been committed the guilt associated with that act normally follows. Satan tries very hard to get us to turn away from God at that very moment. However, God still wants the intimate relationship with us that Jesus provided by the shedding his blood. This is the sole purpose of seeking his face and not just what is in his hand. The scripture in Hebrews chapter 4 verses 16 says it best. It reads, "Let us therefore come boldly unto the throne of grace, that we may obtain mercy, and find grace to help in time of need." In essence, this is what God expects from his children. To turn away from God and not seek his face when repenting is in itself a sin. The next component in the principle of repentance is to turn from our wicked ways. This is any behavior that is against the known will of God. This signifies a 180 degree turn to go in the opposite direction. Notice that each one of the four components is a direct act of the heart. Yes, you guessed it. True repentance is a matter of the heart (your human spirit). Once these have been done in its proper order; and true repentance has taken place from the heart, that's when God does what he has promised. The first thing God will do is hear from heaven. This simply means that he accepts your invitation to get involved in the situation. Next, he will forgive the sin. He will not hold the sin against you. He does this by applying his Son's blood to the situation. He will then heal their land. The word land here can best be interpreted as your heart. He will heal your heart. How does the healing of the heart

happen? God uses the same agent to heal the heart as he does to forgive and wash away the sin. It is by the blood of Jesus. Paul writes to the Hebrews the in-depth answer to the question. It is found in Hebrews 9:13-14. It states, "For if the blood of bulls and of goats, and the ashes of a heifer sprinkling the unclean, sanctifieth to the purifying of the flesh: how much more shall the blood of Christ, who through the eternal Spirit offered himself without spot to God, purge your conscience (your human spirit) from dead works to serve the living God?" Remember it is through true repentance that we demonstrate to God that we are indeed ready to receive the Kingdom of God and all that it entails. The Kingdom Principle of Agreement must first begin with the principle of repentance.

Chapter 10

The Kingdom Principle of Agreement

Overview

The Power of Agreement- This principle states that where two or more touch and agree concerning anything on earth it shall be done for them of the Father.

This makes the union of marriage a powerful entity and gives the married couple and incredible tool for success.

Salvation the Ultimate State of Agreement- Salvation itself requires us to agree with God concerning His son Jesus. That Jesus alone is the way, the truth, and the life and that no man can come unto the Father except by Him.

Agreement Based on Truth and not Popularity- Many of the world's problems exist because we attempt to live by the world's system and not by the principles of the Word. Popularity is not a kingdom principle of God. This understanding makes democracy based on popularity unreliable and ineffective at best.

Divide and Conquer the Weapon of the Enemy- Satan brings division by having the believer question the validity of the word of God. Jesus said, "A house divided against itself cannot stand. This is an important remainder for all marriages.

True Repentance is agreeing with God- A true act of repentance is an act of the heart and the process must be followed as God has outlined in 2 Chronicles 7:14.

CHAPTER 11

The Kingdom Principle Faithfulness

"And the things that thou hast heard of me among many witnesses, the same commit thou to faithful men who shall be able to teach others also." 2 Timothy 2:2

I heard a minister make the statement that longevity is not the only attribute or quality that measures faithfulness. He said, "That donation and not duration is a better telling sign of ones faithfulness." He went on to explain that many of us as believers have adopted the philosophy that as long as we are attending every church function and activity that it somehow makes up for the lack of work that is being done in the church. He was simply saying what the word says, that only the doers of the Word of God are blessed. Because we have been taught in error we often have a hard time converting to the ways of God when they are presented to us in truth. We are still waiting on Jesus to come down from Heaven and physically accomplish for the church what he has already given us the power and authority through his name to accomplish. This has been a very affective weapon for the enemy against the people of God. He makes us believe that meaningless programs to honor the traditions of men are somehow pleasing to the Father without having to commit to the things that He has commanded us to do. Specifically the great commission which commands us to go and compel them to come teaching all nations, baptizing them in the name of the Father, and of the Son, and the Holy Ghost: Teaching them to observe all things whatsoever I have commanded you: and lo, I am with you always, even unto the end of the world. (St. Matthew 28:19-20) This command from the Lord and our willingness to obey it better speaks more of our faithfulness than our years spent inside the church walls observing our traditions.

Faithfulness is …..

My definition of faithfulness is defined as being loyal, committed, attached and a supporter to the perfect will of God. The individual words alone give us a measuring stick as to our level of faithfulness to God and His kingdom assignments. Just as everything in the Word of God causes us to examine our own life, this definition will hopefully do the same for you as well. Let's take a closer look at each word carefully and find out what the Word of God has to say.

It has been said that even criminals have a sense of loyalty for what they believe. Loyalty, as with the other words outlined in the definition, are words of action. Loyalty must be demonstrated to be fully understood. I believe that many can come to grasp the power of loyalty from having experienced the feeling of betrayal. Betrayal is the opposite of loyalty. Jesus during his earthly ministry showed all of mankind through his actions how we are to respond to those who have demonstrated their disloyalty or betrayal. Because loyalty and faithfulness are great kingdom characteristics and speaks volumes about the believer, so does the character of someone who demonstrates disloyalty and betrayal. The scripture states is St Luke 22:47-48, "And while he yet spoke, behold a multitude, and he that was called Judas, one of the twelve, went before them, and drew near unto Jesus to kiss him. But Jesus said unto him, "Judas, betrayest thou the Son of Man with a kiss?" Jesus never responded with hurtful words or actions toward the one who was unfaithful and disloyal. The comfort we have today rests in the understanding that we unlike Judas have a way to make our disloyalty and betrayal to Christ forgiven and washed away. Whenever we sin against the knowledge of the Word of God we betray that innocent blood that redeemed us from the very sin we have gone back to.

The old cliché states that we cannot try to fit God into our lifestyle but God must be our lifestyle. Commitment to God is simply making the things of God your only priority. Jesus said, "...for I do always those things that pleased the Father." (St. John 8:29b) As our example, we must also make pleasing the Father our only priority. To do that we must commit all that we are to Him and His will for us.

The gospel of St. John is a very powerful account of the ministry of Jesus. In chapter 15 Jesus says, "I am the true vine and my Father is the husbandman. Every branch in me that bears not fruit he takes away: and every branch that bears fruit he purges it, that it may bring forth more fruit. Now you are clean through the word which I have spoken unto you. Abide in me and I in you. As the branch cannot bear fruit of itself except it abide in the vine; no more can you, except you abide in me. I am the vine you are the branches: He that abides in me and I in him, the same brings forth much fruit: for without me you can do nothing." As long as we are attached to the source of our being which is Jesus we will produce much fruit. However he clearly states that if we are not attached to Him we can do nothing. What a powerful statement of attachment.

Whatever we support should increase. Because we are only supporting those things pertaining to the will of God we know that it will cause tangible increase in that area. To support is to give of your time, talent and treasure to the things of God. We are to always remember that we are not our own but have been purchased with the precious blood of Jesus. Just imagine what it would be like if all of God's children supported the will of God here on earth. There would be no lack for anyone and we would take our rightful place as true kings and priests here in God's earthly kingdom. This is the true will of God for mankind.

Your faithfulness is measured by God and to God by your loyalty, commitment, attachment and support of his will. Ever wonder how faithful you are? Ask those you were assigned to assist.

Your Faithfulness is not your call

I have come to know that we cannot measure our faithfulness ourselves. Faithfulness can only be measured by those who have been placed in your life as the authority over your life. The ultimate authority is of course Jesus. However we have men and woman who have been given authority over us and they are the ones who can best account for our faithfulness. How we serve others is the true reflection of our loyalty, commitment, attachment and support. In other words, it demonstrates to them our faithfulness.

Jesus also taught the principle to His disciples is St. Luke 16:10-12. He states, "He that is faithful in that which is least is faithful also in much: and he that is unjust in the least is unjust also in much. If therefore, you have not been faithful in the unrighteous mammon, who will commit to your trust the true riches? And if you have not been faithful in that which is another man's, who shall give you that which is your own?" Jesus indicated that we must first show our faithfulness to someone else before God will entrust us with something of our own. This principle understanding has hindered the believer and robbed him of God's best. Satan has the believer thinking that his loyalty, commitment, attachment and support for his family, employer/employees, church, community and God somehow does not factor into the blessing of promotion from God. If you want to be promoted demonstrate to God your faithfulness in serving others. God commands us to do all things as unto the Lord. (Ref. Colossians 3:23) In doing so, we position ourselves to receive the blessings that God has predestined for us to have. Are your promotions in life being held up? Check your loyalty, commitment, attachment and support (faithfulness) to others you have been assigned to serve.

The Conclusion in Judgment

The conclusion in judgment is not and has never been good try my good and unfaithful servant. It is however well done my good and faithful servant. God views our acts of faithfulness as the conclusion in judgment for us. We all want to hear the Lord say those words over our life on that great and notable day. It is equally important for us to demonstrate to those who have authority over us this principle and characteristic of the kingdom of God. Jesus indicated that our promotions come from our demonstration of faithfulness and commitment to the ministry of another. If you are having a hard time trying to figure out where you may stand in this area of your life just ask those who have authority over you and take heed to their responses. Husbands ask your wife where you rate in the area of faithfulness to the things of God. They will tell you. Employees ask your boss for their assessment to your level of faithfulness to the company that employs you. Take a moment and ask your pastor to evaluate your level of faithfulness to the church vision and the will of God. Faithfulness should be one of the many kingdom principles to be exhibited in your daily walk with Christ.

Chapter 11

The Kingdom Principle of Faithfulness

Overview

Faithfulness in the Kingdom of God is defined as being loyal, committed, attached and a supporter to the perfect will of God.

Your faithfulness is not your call. Faithfulness in you is always measured by another. Ask those who are closest to you or those who have authority over your life to evaluate your level of faithfulness.

The conclusion in judgment has always been and will always be well done my good and faithful servant. Only the doers of the Word of God are blessed.

CHAPTER 12

The Kingdom Principle of Prayer

"And this is the confidence we have in him, that, if we ask anything according to his will, he hears us: and if we know that he hears us, whatsoever we ask, we know that we have the petitions that we desire of him." 1 John 5:14-15

During one of my mentors many incredible teachings he began to speak on the subject of prayer. He stated that, "if the children of God believed that their prayers would be answered they would always pray." The statement resonated with me as well as the others who were as interested in what he had to say. I began to think later about his statement and concluded that he was absolutely correct. If we really believed that our prayer would be answered we would always seek the face of God for what we desired. However one of the key reasons we fail to come before God with our concerns is we don't have a total confidence in our ability to get our prayers answered. Before I understood the dynamics of prayer, its effectiveness and power I was guilty of not having the kind of prayer life God requires us to have. From a child I heard all of the church clichés that said God will only give you what you need and not what you want. I was a victim to the statements that said "Sometimes God will answer yes and sometimes he will answer no and sometimes he will answer wait awhile." I never thought that those older ministers were misled themselves. After learning the truth about our foundational scripture in 1 John 5:14-15, I came to know that the answers to all of your prayers to God are indeed yes. There is however a condition that must first be met.

Three things to remember concerning prayer

When we pray we must have a complete understanding of these three things in order to be effective in our prayers. The first thing is we must remember that **God is the source of our prayers**. In St. John 16:23 Jesus says, "And in that day you shall ask me nothing. Verily, verily, I say unto you, whatsoever you shall ask the Father in my name, he will give it to you." Jesus teaches because the Father is the source of our prayers we must ask Him in the name of Jesus. Second we must remember that **Jesus is the mediator of our prayers**. Hebrews 12:24 says, "And to Jesus the mediator of the new covenant…." A mediator is one who goes before and represents for both parties and serves as a go between to make sure that all parties involved receive the benefits of what is in the covenant agreement. And third **the Holy Spirit is the intercessor for our prayers**. I have come to know concerning prayer that there is not a lack of ability just a lack of understanding. Romans 8:26-27 states, "Likewise the Spirit also helps our infirmities: for we know not what to pray for as we ought: but the Spirit itself makes intercession for us with groaning which cannot be uttered. And he that searches the hearts knows the mind of the Spirit, because he makes intercession for the saints according to the will of God." The Holy Spirit is the only person that knows the mind of the Father here on earth. It is the assignment of the Holy Spirit to teach you about your purpose and the will of God concerning your life. When we go before God in prayer we are to remember, just as Jesus taught us, to seek and request that God's will be done and not our own. The Holy Spirit when we yield to him tells us of the will of God for every situation. Jesus told the disciples that He would not leave them comfortless. He also told them that He would pray to the Father and the Father would send them another Comforter even the Spirit of truth who would abide with them forever.

In the scriptures the Lord refers to the Holy Spirit of God by four distinct names. He addressed him as:

1. The Comforter
2. The Spirit of Truth
3. The Teacher
4. The Guide

The Comforter

The Lord referred to the Holy Spirit as the Comforter because he was to provide the same level of comfort and security that Jesus provided for His disciples while He was with them. As long as Jesus was with them they had no worries or concerns about their life. The King of Glory was there to provide everything they needed both naturally as well as spiritually. Right before Jesus departed He needed to calm the disciples fear. They had grown to trust in the Lord with their very lives and did not want to loose that security they had found in Jesus. The Lord assured them that The Comforter which will come from The Father would be present with them at all times reminding them of the things that He had taught and commanded. He taught them the Holy Spirit would provide the same level of comfort and security that He had provided for them and they could trust in the Holy Spirit of God the same way they trusted in the Son of God.

The Spirit of Truth

When God was asked by Moses what is your name, God responded by saying, "I AM." This statement gives us a clear understanding of what the Lord meant by calling the Holy Spirit the Spirit of Truth. Jesus said that God is love, not that he merely possesses love but His very being is love. And so it is with everything that exists. The Holy Spirit is truth not that he possess truth but He is truth. When the Spirit of God speaks he can only speak truth because that is what He is. Jesus assured the disciples that the Holy Spirit would guide them into all truth and righteousness. The Holy Spirit not only provides the comfort of God's security and purpose but he also represents the truth of God's word by bearing witness of Jesus who is the way the truth and the life.

The Teacher

Whenever you are the first of something by default you are its teacher. One of the most important assignments the Holy Spirit has is to teach you about The Kingdom of God and your purpose within the Kingdom here on Earth. As Jesus ministered, he spoke consistently about the Kingdom of God and its right understanding. The Holy Spirit since the departure of the Lord is the teacher of the Kingdom. When Jesus was here on Earth he expressly taught the disciples about God's Kingdom using many parables that related to their everyday life. The Holy Spirit is the only one that knows the mind of God here on Earth and is therefore the only qualified instructor of God's perfect will. It is his responsibility by assignment to teach us about The Kingdom of God and its King by using the Word of God and its principles along with our own experiences.

The Guide

The remaining name that Jesus called the Holy Spirit was the guide. He will guide us into all truth and righteousness. Notice the scripture teaches that he will guide us and not force us. God will never force mankind to serve Him. It is done of our own free will. A guide is someone who goes before you to show you the way. The Holy Spirit does just that for all of mankind. Whether you are saved and have been redeemed by the blood of Jesus or have not yet received Him as your savior, the Holy Spirit has been given to guide you to Him. Jesus indicated that the Holy Spirit would not speak of himself but would bear witness of the Son of God.

According to His will

One of the key elements of prayer is found in verse 14 of our foundational scripture. It indicates that all of our prayers must be according to His will. Because our life should be lived according to God's divine will we can be confident that He will never call us to a set of objectives and then withhold the resources we need to get the job done. That is one of my mentor's favorite sayings. To get your prayer answered you must pray in accordance with the will of God for the situation. The scripture is so important to us that it gives the road map to answered prayers. The children of God have everything they need to know the will of God and to pray accordingly. The written word of God (the Bible) tells us of His will. The Son of God (Jesus) came as the expressed image of God to show us the will of the Father. The Holy Spirit has been given to reveal the mind of God to us and to guide us with His will. The reason the answer to all of mans prayer are yes is because God will not hear any prayer that is not according to his will. The key is to always pray the will of God because that is what the Father will respond to. If it is not according to His will he will not hear it. The confidence that comes with knowing His will is what causes us to ask in faith and to believe that we have received the moment we pray. Thus giving us full assurance that what we ask for will be done for us of the Father. If we know the will of God we are totally confident in our request to Him. God the Father has assured us that whatsoever we ask according to His will He will do it for us. He cannot deny His own will. Effective prayer is always in line with the will of God which is found in His word.

Different kinds of Prayer

The word of God gives us to know that there are different kinds of prayer. Just as there are different kinds of trees and all have the same fundamental function, so prayer has different applications but the same ultimate goal. That is to invite God into the situation so that His will is established and the outcome he desires prevails.

One of the most common types of prayer is the prayer of petition. This kind of prayer asks God for something. This is also the prayer that most believers have a hard time with. As I stated earlier this prayer requires that you know the will of God for your life. I have found that many who are still growing in the knowledge of God and His will have yet to understand that they really don't have to pray for the things they need. God has promised to take care of all of their needs. Food, shelter, clothing and water the Father provides all that you will need daily. Jesus gave us the perfect example when He referenced the birds of the air. He said that they don't sow or reap but God feeds them daily. Then he asked the question, "Aren't you not much more than they?" (St. Matthew 6:26)

Philippians 4:6-7 says, "Be careful for nothing; but in everything by prayer and supplication with thanksgiving let your request be made know unto God. And the peace of God which passes all understanding, shall keep your hearts and minds through Christ Jesus."

The Prayer of Supplication

It had seemed as if I were in this particular storm for an unusual amount of time. I had suffered the loss of resources as well as time. The storm was beginning to take its toll on me financially, mentally and spiritually as well. I took my concern before God in prayer and waited for the answer. As I was about to get up from my prayer position the Spirit of the Lord spoke and quoted the above scripture. He said, "Be careful for nothing; but in everything by prayer and supplication with thanksgiving let your request be made known unto God. And the peace of God which passes all understanding, shall keep your hearts and mind through Christ Jesus." At first I thought that He was reassuring me that my request had been heard and my petition had been granted. However, throughout the day and the following days the Spirit of God would bring back to my mind the scripture. To my surprise the storm not only continued but it intensified. I went back before the Lord again after recounting in my mind the prayer of faith. I was sure I believed I had received at the moment I prayed. Even after repeated attempts there was no change in the situation. The Lord spoke to me again the same scripture. As the storm intensified I grew frustrated and a bit angry that the manifestation had not taken place. At this point during prayer I ask the Lord to reveal to me why the manifestation had not come. With a firm, clear, soft voice the Spirit spoke and said, "My son, you think you know what the scripture really means and you don't." He said, "Go back and study it." During the course of the day I began to study the scripture and to dissect its meaning and sure enough I was in error of what it really meant. The beginning of the scripture says, "Be careful for nothing." This simply means don't worry about anything. The next part of the verse says, "But in everything by prayer and supplication with thanksgiving let your requests be made known unto God." In everything by prayer means in everything worship, the word prayer the way that it is used here means too "worship." The mystery in what the Spirit was saying was found in the next word, supplication. As I researched the word I found its meaning. Supplication means written petition. At that moment the revelation came. God was commanding me to write out my petition. He instructed me to find the scriptures that applied to my situation and write them in the form of a prayer and present them back to him. He simply was commanding that I give Him back His word. The final part was to do it with thanksgiving. He reminded me that you thank someone for having done something for you after they have done it. This was to demonstrate that I understood that He had already granted my request. Wow! There it was the answer to my prayer of why I had not received the manifestation and why the storm had not ceased. Hear the promises in verse 7, "And the peace of God, which passes all understanding, shall keep your hearts and minds through Christ Jesus." I was not experiencing peace because I had not done what the scripture required to have it. As I studied I realized that a petition is a legal document. I took the time to write out the petition as a legal document equipped with the written scriptures that corresponded with what I was asking God to do for me. Once the petition was finished I sat down and prayed the Word of God back to the Father as I had written it. This time there was a distinct difference in my faith. I was totally confident that my request had been granted. At that very moment I felt a peace that I could not explain. The very next day I began to see the manifestation of what I had asked for. The storm was over, financial misfortunes had been reversed and I had a renewed faith. From that day until this day I am still experiencing the benefits of that written out prayer of supplication.

The reason we can be confident when we pray and not have to worry is because we understand that God will watch over his Word to perform it. When we pray according to His will, we can rest in the assurance that what we pray for will be done for us. God encourages us to come before Him with our prayers and requests and to come to Him with thanksgiving. Thanksgiving is an acknowledgement of things that have already been done. God will always search the hearts of His children to determine what the motives behind your requests are. When we petition God we should also tell God what we want as well as why we want it. Since everything in life was created and made to benefit something outside of itself God is waiting to hear how others will benefit form your request. One of the key factors in petition prayer is we must pray based on the Word of God and the promises He has made to us. Because all of the promises of God are received by faith, we can only hinge our faith and requests on the promises He has made. For example, I have a right to go to God for healing because that is apart of His promise to His children. I have confidence in the knowledge of His Word that tells me that by Jesus stripes we were healed. (Ref 1 Peter 2:24)

The Whole Armor of God is made complete with prayer

When I gained a revelation of the Whole Armor of God found in the book of Ephesians chapter 6, I was pleased to know that the armor contained six pieces; however the entirety of the armor and its applications are not complete until verse 18 of that same chapter has been added. The Word of God states in verse 18, "Praying always with all prayer and supplication in the Spirit, and watching thereunto with perseverance and supplication for all saints." As a young minister I have often heard this preached from a selfish standpoint. Not that the preachers were trying to harm or misinform, they were just preaching what they themselves had been taught. The meaning for the whole armor of God was not only for you as a believer on the battlefield of life but your armor is for the underdeveloped saints and nonbelievers who are not quite aware that they are in a spiritual battle for their eternal soul. God requires that you put on the whole armor, found in Ephesians 6:13-18, so that you are equipped to handle all of the challenges that you will face during this battle. Because the battle will last as long as you live you must be taught how to use it correctly. It will not only protect you but others as well. It is the responsibility of the believer who understands why he has his armor and how to use it to watch with perseverance and supplication for all saints. When I was traveling recently the Lord brought this understanding to me and made it crystal clear using the instructions of the flight attendant on the plane. When the attendant came to the part that said in case of an emergency and the cabin looses pressure and is not able to manage the air flow, oxygen masks will drop from the over head compartment to assist in the management of air intake. When the attendant came to the part that said if you are traveling with a small child, in case of this emergency make sure you secure your mask first and then assist the child with theirs. It was at that moment I gained a complete understanding of the importance of the armor and the reason for it. If you as a strong believer have the armor on and are effectively using it, you know that you cannot help others until your armor is secured first. The true test of whether we can use the whole armor effectively lies in verse 18 that commands us to watch and pray for all saints with perseverance. As I have said many times, "Everything in life was created and made to benefit something outside of itself, even the whole armor of God."

Intercessory Prayer

I stated earlier that the Holy Spirit of God was given to be our intercessor. An intercessor is someone who intervenes on our behalf because they have a greater understanding and knowledge than we have. This function was assigned to the Holy Spirit of God by the Father. Jesus himself during his time on Earth served as the intercessor for the disciples. The scripture teach us that we are to conform to the will of God by having the mind of Christ. The mind of Christ on Earth was to always do the will of the Father and to intercede on behalf of the world that didn't have the knowledge or understanding that Jesus the Son of God possessed. It is our commandment that we intercede on behalf of our family and friends and to ultimately extend that to the whole world. As believers our greatest joy should be to see a person who was once lost come to the saving grace and knowledge of the Lord and to gain the salvation that has been provided and to learn how to live according to the Word of God. If this is our greatest joy than our greatest sorrow must be to see mankind exist outside of Gods will and to die without receiving Christ as their savior. My mentor asked the congregation of our church this question, "How many people have come to the Lord because of your prayers and direct actions of love toward them?" Every since that question pierced my heart I have intentionally established and set my spiritual goals every year to include how many people I will directly lead to Christ for that year. One of the ways we can look at intercessory prayer is to view your self as the one that God has assigned to come before Him on their behalf. Have you ever had a pressing in your spirit to drop all that you were doing and to pray for an individual? When this occurs, it is the Holy Spirit of God speaking to you to invoke the assistance of God for them. Whenever there is a situation that you just can't seem to get out of your spirit, this is a perfect indication of God's presence inviting you to seek Him on your behalf and the behalf of others.

For those of you who have an established prayer life I encourage you to make a list of those the Lord instructs you to pray for. As you obey God you will notice the list growing on a continuous basis. He will continue to add more and more people to that list. Count it a privilege that God trust you to intercede on behalf of those who may not be as strong in the faith at that moment. I have been very blessed to see my youngest brother; my sister and mother all come to Christ because of intentional intercessory prayers. The word of God teaches us that the effectual fervent prayer of a righteous man avails much. (Ref. James 5:16b) As a believer we have the right to expect God to deliver those that we intercede for from the bondage that holds them captive whether it's spiritual, physical or mental.

The Faith Prayer

Two of my favorite scriptures are found in the book of Philippians chapter 4 verses 6 and St. Mark 11:24 it says, "Be careful for nothing; but in everything by prayer and supplication with thanksgiving let your requests be made know unto God." Mark 11:24 says, "Therefore I say unto you, what things soever you desire, when you pray, believe that you receive them, and you shall have them." As a young boy in the sixth grade, Mrs. Koch's class to be exact, I remember her giving away this particular object in class. She indicated that she would give it randomly to who ever she chose. I remember wanting that object really badly. I closed my eyes and asked God in an open prayer to please let me be the one she chose. When I opened my eyes Mrs. Koch was standing just a few steps from my desk. As she moved a few steps closer my heart seemed as if it would melt because of the warm peaceful feeling that came over me. When she handed me the object my heart was overwhelmed. Not because of the object only, but because I was sure that God had answered me and made this happen for me.

Since that time I have come to understand and value my prayer life. It is the essence of invoked power. My mentor says, "Little prayer little power, much prayer much power and no prayer no power." How true that is. Just like all of the principles of God, petition prayers must contain several things in order to be answered. We have learned that prayer must be according to the will of God no matter what kind of prayer it is. We also learned that prayer must be based on a promise from God either written in the Bible or spoken by the Holy Spirit and you must have a Godly reason or pure motive behind your request. Very few believers ever challenge God through prayer. We as believers live with our desires unmet never really knowing His will for our lives. The Word of God teaches us that through prayer and supplication with thanksgiving we are to make our request known to God. So remember when you pray tell God what you want and why you want it and how it will bless others. I have found that the prayer of faith contains a process that assures me the manifestation of my prayer. The process says that I must say what I want, believe in my heart at the time I am praying not doubting that I have received it and I shall have it. In other words, I must ask, believe and receive what I have asked for at the time I pray. This is the prayer of faith. The last thing that must be remembered is found in St Mark 11: 25-26 it says, "And when you stand praying, forgive, if you have aught against any; that your Father also which is in heaven may forgive you your trespasses. But if you do not forgive, neither will your Father which is in heaven forgive your trespasses." Your heart must remain clean from any un forgiveness, this will clear the way for you to receive what you have asked for.

7 Dynamics of the Lord's Prayer

For most children one of the earliest recognitions of the presence of God is being taught the Lord's Prayer. Just as children who grow up in a household where the Word of God is not a top priority, many believers are familiar with the prayer but are not aware of its meaning. St Matthew 6: 9-13 gives us the pattern prayer spoken by our Lord and Savior Jesus Christ. He states, "After this manner therefore pray ye: Our father which art in heaven, Hallowed be thy name. Thy kingdom come. Thy will be done in earth, as it is in heaven. Give us this day our daily bread. And forgive us our debts, as we forgive our debtors. And lead us not into temptation, but deliver us from evil; for thine is the kingdom, and the power, and the glory, for ever. Amen." Let's take a look at all seven dynamics of this incredible prayer.

1. Our Father- This addresses God the Father as the source and sustainer of all that we hope to gain in Him. The word father also addresses and makes reference to His relationship to us and not our relationship to Him. He is our Father first and not we His children first. Fathers

always precedes the children. It is a great reminder of His love and commitment to us.

2. Hallowed be thy name- This addresses the attention of the prayer toward God and reverence for His name and His person. Hallowed means to hold in reverence and holy awe.

3. Thy kingdom come- The Kingdom represents the full and effective reign of God through Jesus Christ here on earth. Let God reign throughout the earth the same way that He reins in heaven. The fullness and true essence of God which includes all of the fruits of the Spirit and all of His laws, precepts, principles and power.

4. Thy will be done- This emphasizes that the idea of prayer is to bring about the conformity of the will of the believer to the will of God. Prayer is an act of spiritual expression that brings us into conformity to the very nature and purpose of God.

5. Give us this day our daily bread- This begins the prayer of faith. Asking God to provide even the essence of food daily. The spiritual connotation fits perfectly with the Old Testament supply of manna from heaven. God provided for the children of Israel daily without their help. God provided manna everyday for the Israelites while they wandered in the wilderness.

6. Forgive us our debts as we forgive our debtors- This refers to our sins, which are moral and spiritual debts to God's righteousness. The request for forgiveness of sins is made by

the believer. It also encompasses the forgiveness of others also.

7. Lead us not into temptation- This is our daily plea to God to intervene at the moment we are tempted with sin. We must always remember that it is not God who tempts with sin. As the scripture teaches us in James 1:13-15, "Let no man say when he is tempted, I am tempted of God: for God cannot be tempted with evil, neither tempts he any man: but every man is tempted, when he is drawn away of his own lusts and enticed." When lust is conceived it brings about sin and when sin is finished it brings about death, a separation from God. The bible wants us to clearly understand this. God will test us to prove our faithfulness to Him. God promises that if we resist the devil he will flee from us.

The conclusions in the text of Matthew 6:13 say, "For thine is the kingdom, the power, and the glory, for ever. Amen" This teaches that at the conclusion of our prayers we are to make a declaration of the source of our prayers and to acknowledge that we are asking for what benefits the kingdom of God, what demonstrates the power of God and what will bring glory to God forever. As the scripture teaches only those things we do for Christ will last.

Chapter 12

The Kingdom Principle of Prayer

Overview

Three (3) things to remember concerning prayer:

1. God is the source of our prayers
2. Jesus is the mediator of our prayers
3. The Holy Spirit is the Intercessor of our prayers

There are (4) distinct names of the Holy Spirit

1. The Comforter
2. The Spirit of Truth
3. The Teacher
4. The Guide

Prayer must be according to the will of God

There are different kinds of prayer

The Whole Armor of God is made complete through prayer

Intercessory Prayer/ The Prayer of Supplication/ Faith Prayer

(7) Dynamics of the Lord's Prayer- The Model Prayer

CHAPTER 13

The Kingdom Principle of Wisdom

"If any of you lack wisdom, let him ask of God, that gives to all men liberally, and upbraideth not; and it shall be given him" James 1:5

"Wisdom is the principle thing; therefore get wisdom: and with all thy getting get understanding." Proverbs 4:7

In the Kingdom of God we are taught to forget those things that are behind us and to look forward and to press toward the mark of a high calling in Christ Jesus. However the world is not so kind as to let us forget our many mistakes along the way. It was at one of those times when my past mistakes were being thrust back into the forefront of my mind that I began to realize that God is not in the business of condemnation and the attack must be coming from the enemy. As I picked up the Word of God to gain some encouragement I came across the scripture in Deuteronomy 31:19 it states, "I call heaven and earth to record this day against you, that I have set before you life and death, blessings and cursing: therefore choose life, that both thou and thy seed may live:" I concluded in my mind that with the help of the Holy Spirit I would strive to always choose life. As I rested in the comfort of the Word of God the Spirit of God revealed to me that choosing the Word, the Will and the Way of God is what true wisdom really is.

Just as God commanded the children of Israel to choose life, He has so instructed us also to choose. As believers we sometimes fail to realize that making the correct choices are the single most important thing that we can do to affect our quality of life. Nothing in life begins until you make a choice and nothing good in life is sustained until you make the right choice for God. The more I began to meditate and ask God for direction in writing this chapter the more He impressed upon me that I could not expound upon the kingdom principle unless the people were aware that wisdom, knowledge and understanding must be taught together. This kingdom principle must be viewed as a three legged easel. If one of the legs is missing the easel will not stand. Therefore it is of the greatest importance that you understand the principle of wisdom in concert with the principle of knowledge and understanding.

Wisdom, Knowledge and Understanding

Since the kingdom of God represents God's laws, statutes, and principles and it is God's will that we choose life, we can be confident in my definition of wisdom that states, "Wisdom is the ability to choose the correct Godly principle for the situation you are facing." "Knowledge is God's revealed truth." "Understanding is the ability to know how to use the principle for maximum impact and results." This gives us a clear understanding why we should not attempt to separate the three.

Wisdom

The ability to choose the correct Godly principle for the situation you are in, gives you the advantage that allows you to overcome any obstacle you may face. In the book of Romans chapter 1 verse 20 the word of God states, "For the invisible things of him from the creation of the world are clearly seen, being understood by the things that are made, even his eternal power and God-head; so that they are without excuse." This particular passage tells us that we can understand spiritual things by observing how natural things work. The principles of God both natural and spiritual all share the same (4) characteristics. They are:

1. Principles work 100% of the time
2. Principles have no respect of person
3. Principles can be violate but never broken
4. Once you understand a principle you can predict its outcome

Having this knowledge helps the believer in their faith walk and allows them to face challenges with true confidence in the Word of God. Let's take a look at how this affects our spiritual understanding. The principle of mathematics will demonstrate the (4) characteristics mentioned above. If I were to ask a room of 5th graders what would be the answer to the math problem of two plus two they would all answer 4. Even if the students attended different schools they would all be able to come to the same conclusion because they were all taught the same mathematical principle of addition. They didn't get the answer because they new it. They were able to come up with the answer because they knew the principle of addition. If they use the same addition principle they should be able to come up with the correct answer every time even if the numbers change and increase in numerical size. If the children of God understood the principles of God it wouldn't matter how large the situation appeared they would still be able to overcome it because the principles work 100% of the time. The principle of addition also has no respect of person. If a 5th grader from Illinois used the principle it would work for them as well as a student from Michigan. The principle can be violated but never broken indicates that the addition can be done incorrectly producing an incorrect answer however the addition principle remain the same. Once the addition principle is understood coming up with the correct answer is easily predicted.

"If any man lacks wisdom (the ability to choose the correct principle for the situation you are facing) let him ask God who gives to all men liberally (freely) and upbraideth not; and it shall be given to him." This principle is found in the book of James 1:5. Wisdom also encompasses why the trials exist and how we are to endure until the manifested change comes. God is committed to his children's continued understanding of how the kingdom of God works. He says that he will freely give you the correct principle to use when faced with a challenge. How awesome is that?

Knowledge

Knowledge is simply God's revealed truth. Since God is truth, anytime we accept the truth of God we are increasing in knowledge. This was evident in the book of Matthew chapter 16:13-17. Jesus asked his disciples, saying, "Who do men say that I the Son of man am?" His disciples answered with various answers however it was Peter in verse 16 that gave them the revealed truth. "And Simon Peter answered and said, Thou art the Christ, the Son of the living God." Verse 17 states, "And Jesus answered and said unto him, blessed art thou, Simon Bar-jona: for flesh and blood has not revealed it unto thee, but my Father which is in heaven." Jesus tells the disciples that the truth of who He was had been revealed unto Peter by the Father. This truth revealed or knowledge gained helped anchor the disciples for their future assignment which was to declare the gospel of the Kingdom of God through Jesus Christ unto all nations.

Understanding

Understanding is to know how to apply the revealed truth or knowledge you have gained. In the chapter entitled the Kingdom principle of Faith I discuss that faith is hearing the word, understanding the word, believing the word and applying the word of God. The Lord revealed to me the importance of understanding when He was teaching me this definition. The Spirit of God ministered this understanding to me. He indicated that many believers are trying to live by faith but are missing a key element in the faith walk and that is the understanding component of faith. How can you have faith for something you don't understand? After you have heard the Word of God you must understand it, once you understand it you can then believe it and once you believe it you can then apply it. That's what the scripture means when it says, "The just shall live by faith." One of the most important teachings in the Bible is the parable of the sower. In St. Matthew chapter 13 Jesus teaches His disciples about the parable of the sower. He says in verse 19, "When any one hears the word of the kingdom, and understands it not, then cometh the wicked one, and catches away that which was sown in his heart. This is he that receives seed by the way side." Satan is always looking for the believer who does not understand the word of God because it is at that point that he can steal it from them. Because they don't understand it they cannot believe it and therefore are most likely not to do it. Remember only the doer of the Word of God is blessed. You must understand it before you will ever live by it consistently.

You do greatly err...

One of the many wonderful things about God is that He knows everything about us and we know very little about Him but he still wants us in His presence. During one of my many Father to son talks I asked God, "Why was there so much hurt and pain in the world." He answered me when I was reading in St. Matthew chapter 22:29. As Jesus was answering a question posed by the Sadducees concerning the resurrection, He said to them, "Ye do err, not knowing the scriptures, nor the power of God." The Holy Spirit ministered this revelation to me. We make mistakes and live out side of the will of God for only two reasons in life. Every mistake ever committed is because of one or the other of these. We make mistakes because we don't know the scriptures or what the Bible says about what we are facing. The second reason is because we don't really know the power of God. Take a moment and think back on every mistake that you have ever made and it will fall into one of these two categories. If we willfully sin it is because we don't really understand the scriptures and if we willfully sin and we know what the word of God says then it is because we really don't know the power of God.

You were created to solve problems

Without a correct understanding of God and His purpose for our life we will sometimes view problems as an intruder and not recognize the true reason we are facing them. As believers we are sometimes guilty of wanting life to be as comfortable as possible and we never realize that it is at the moment of confrontation we have to exercise our potential for growth. It has been said that we grow more out of facing problem than we do from enjoying blessings. I am a living testimony of that. When God created you before the foundation of the world He had a specific purpose in mind. In other words He has a specific problem or problems He wants you to face and overcome. In doing so you not only get the rewards of what solving the problem brings you position yourself for an even greater promotion. Jesus stated, "If you are faithful over a few things God will make you ruler over many." Even in the worlds system this kingdom principle is practiced. I have found out that through this principle you can gain promotion even in the secular world. Find out what problem your supervisor has and solve it. Find out what problem your client has and solve it. People who solve problems are rewarded handsomely for it. The better you are at solving problems the greater the task you will be entrusted with. There are always two types of people, those who solve problems and receive the rewards or those that create them for other to solve. Whenever I am asked to listen and then evaluate what others may deem a problem I am always listening to determine whether their concern falls into the category of an actual problem or not. Many times we mislabel what I call a fact of life as a problem. A fact of life is something that is beyond your control. For example, being born blind is a fact of life and not a problem. Not having sight is a fact of life however not having vision is a problem. Whenever we are faced with a fact of life we simply have to adjust our attitude concerning it. It becomes difficult at times to see the errors of our own ways through our own way of thinking and that is one of the primary reasons we are to know what the Word of God has to say concerning the challenges we will face. Choosing the correct principle to solve the problems that are before us gives us the assurance that the outcome will be beneficial to everyone involved. God created you to solve problems using the kingdom principle of wisdom by doing so you will bring healing and wholeness to those you are serving, reward and recognition to yourself and glory to God the Father.

Chapter 13

The Kingdom Principle of Wisdom

Overview

Wisdom- The ability to choose the correct Kingdom principle for the situation you are facing.

Knowledge- It is God's revealed truth

Understanding- Is how to use or apply the Kingdom Principle

Wisdom, knowledge and understanding must always be taught together. They stand together as a three legged easel.

You do greatly err.... We only make mistakes in life for two reasons:

1. Not knowing the scriptures
2. Not knowing the power of God

You were created to solve problems- The challenges you face are a perfect backdrop for God to work through you. Those who solve problems are promoted and paid handsomely for it.

Problems are not intruders but opportunities

CHAPTER 14

The Kingdom Principle of Judging

"Judge not, that ye be not judged. For with what judgment ye judge, ye shall be judged: and with what measure ye mete, it shall be measured to you again." St. Matthew 7:1-2

As a young man I have always been concerned about the feelings of others. I grew up in a culture where playing the dozens was a common activity among the people in my neighborhood. Playing the dozens (for those who may not be aware) means to insult another with a sharp wit; to putdown another and make yourself look good at their expense. Usually insults about their clothing, hair style, hygiene and overall appearance. Those who were good at the dozens were esteemed very highly in the neighborhood. We had some guys who were really good at insulting others. Usually during a crowded session at the basketball court or one of the hang out spots is where you would find several people engaged in a fierce battle. I learned a lot about people and their behavior while watching these battles. I noticed that the people who were good at insulting others were often times the ones who were the most insecure. They were the ones who initiated the confrontation of words because they were afraid that they would soon be the one attacked by someone else. Even though those situations were cruel and often led to physical confrontations they continued everyday for as long as I could remember. When I began to analyze the many battles I had witnessed over the years I was often saddened by the need of someone to insult another for the sake of feeling better about their self. It was always puzzling to me why they couldn't say something positive and uplift the other person with their words as opposed to criticizing and reinforcing the low self esteem many already lived with. As I came into the knowledge of the kingdom principle of judging and the impact that words have I realized that this to was a spiritual weapon of the enemy.

Judge not…

Our foundational scripture was spoken by our Lord Jesus as a principle of the Word of God. He makes it very clear that we are not to condemn, complain, curse or criticize what God has created. A person's clothing, hair style and over all appearance is not an indicator of their true value and worth. To judge another is to say that we are aware of the true intent of their heart. Jesus says, if we judge our judgment is not just. Simply because we do not have the ability to look into the heart of a person and determine for sure what their motives are. Only God possesses that ability. Because God (the Trinity) is the only one that can see into the heart of man He is the only one qualified to judge justly. When we judge another we are using our standard of what we believe and not God's command of not judging to view others. Jesus is our standard measuring stick. It is the image of Jesus that God is shaping and molding us into and not the image of one another. The scripture teaches that if we judge another we will be judged in the same area where we have passed judgment. This principle is easily understood by the question of, "Have you ever spoken evil (an untruth) against someone else?" The answer is of course yes. The next question is, "Has anyone ever spoken evil (an untruth) about you?" Romans chapter 2 verse 1 states this principle clearly. It says, "Therefore thou art inexcusable, O man, whosoever thou art that judges: for where in thou judgest another, thou condemnest thyself; for thou that judgest doeth the same things."

One of the other truths hidden in this principle has to do with the seeds of un forgiveness and bitterness. Whenever we judge another we sow a seed into our own spirit that will reproduce after its own kind. Just as it is in the natural planting of seeds the spiritual planting of seeds produces what has been sown also. When we sow seeds of judgment against another we will harvest seeds of judgment against ourselves. The same is true concerning the seeds of bitterness. When we sow that seed we will reap a harvest of bitterness. Whatever we judge in our hearts concerning another we will be judged in that same area. Many of the heart aches we endure are a direct result of having judged another. Whether we are aware or unaware we are experiencing the spiritual law and its consequences.

The same measure you mete...

This part of the principle can best be explained this way. Because the principles of God govern the kingdom of God all believers are subject to its laws whether you are aware of them or not. In the book of James chapter 2 verse 13 James writes. "For he shall have judgment without mercy, that have showed no mercy; and mercy rejoices against judgment." Here we see that if a person shows no mercy towards his fellow man, he will be judged by the ultimate judge without any mercy. With the same measure that is used to judge others is the same measure that will be used to judge you by God. That is why a person who harbors un forgiveness in their heart cannot receive forgiveness from God. He must measure back to you using the same measure you used. Ask yourself; are their others I have placed an unjust judgment on? Are their others I need to ask for forgiveness from? If so take the opportunity now while the Spirit of God is ministering to you and go and make that relationship right before the Lord that you may receive forgiveness also.

Love unqualified

It may be hard to understand that in many cases we look at others as them having to qualify for our love. As I indicated in the chapter on the kingdom principle of love, I stated that love is the intrinsic desire and unconditional commitment to meet another persons needs, even if that means going above and beyond your initial expectations. What does a person have to do to qualify for your love? If there is an answer other than nothing we are sitting in the seat of judgment. One of the crucial and most difficult things I had to master was this one. The Lord spoke this to my spirit to give me an understanding of how I was to view all people. He said, "How someone treats you should ever determine how you treat them." As I reflected on what had been spoken to my spirit I quickly concluded that this is the meaning of unconditional love. I have lived from that day to this one with that understanding in my heart. Every time and in every situation I am reminded that it is not the person but the enemy that influences that person to mistreat others. I must see them as God sees them, as someone who by their very actions and words is crying out for deliverance and help. Jesus stated that, "God is love." Therefore you and I are love because we came out of Him. We are the very essence of what He is. To judge another is to deny the very essence of who they are and the source they originated from. No one should have to qualify to receive what you really are. One of your true purposes is to advantage and benefit something and someone outside of your self. In essence judging is seeing someone as not having the same value and worth as you.

A Prayer for freedom from judging

Heavenly Father, I thank you for your love and everlasting mercy. I come to you asking that you help me see others as you see them. And to respond to them out of the love of Jesus that you have placed in my heart. Father, help me to respond to life with the compassion of Jesus. Forgive me for my fault finding and judgmental attitude even the belief that I am serving you as one who has the most truth. Forgive me for my wrong actions toward others and my wrong beliefs of who you are and who I am in you. Thank you Father for cleansing me from all unrighteousness and I receive your forgiveness right now in the name of our Lord and Savior Jesus Christ. Amen

Chapter 14

The Kingdom Principle of Judging

Chapter Overview

Judging- Is seeing others as not having the same value and worth as you.

Judge not- Jesus commands us not to judge because our judgment is not just. God (Trinity) is the only one who has the ability to know what is in the heart of another. He alone is the discerner of the hearts of men.

The same measure ye mete- God says that we will be judged with same measure that we used to judge others. This is why God will not forgive you until you have forgiven others.

Love unqualified- No one should have to qualify for your love. The essence of God is love therefore because man came out of God we are love also. God expects you to give what you are to benefit others.

A Prayer for freedom from judging

CHAPTER 15

The Kingdom Principle of Sacrifice

"Greater love hath no man than this that a man lay down his life for his friends" St John 15:13

"I will freely sacrifice unto thee: I will praise thy name O Lord; for it is good." Psalms 54:6

I was finishing a bible study class when one of the regular church members approached me and asked me a question of why life had presented itself as a challenge that she seemingly couldn't bare. After asking her to clarify what she meant she indicated that life had taken a turn for the worst. Not just in a particular area but in all areas of her life. She was convinced that the presence and anointing of God had left and was not operational in her life. She talked about her past victories with God and the closeness she once felt. I could see in her eyes the pain of someone who was searching for something she had lost. Not having the closeness she once enjoyed with God was causing her faith to wane. While she was speaking the Spirit of God revealed these words to me. He said,

"The sacrifice is not acceptable to me." I was immediately reminded of the scripture in the book of Romans chapter 12 verse 1 which says, "I beseech you therefore by the mercies of God, that you present your bodies a living sacrifice, holy, acceptable unto God, which is your reasonable service." When she finished speaking I revealed to her what I had heard. I pointed out that whenever we yield our bodies as an instrument of unrighteousness we become slaves to the one who is the author of unrighteousness. She lowered her head and began to speak very slowly. After acknowledging that the words that were spoken to her were accurate we prayed and asked God for forgiveness and she repented for her actions. Later during the course of one of the classes she had a wonderful testimony of how God's anointing was again present in her life. The act of presenting your body as a living sacrifice indicates that God just as He did in the Old Testament still requires a sacrifice from us. When we present our bodies as living sacrifices we demonstrate to God our willingness to worship Him as He commanded.

The Lord quickly reminded me that He is under no obligation to accept a sacrifice that is not presented to Him as holy. Often times we forget that when we come before the King of Glory we must come before Him with a pure heart and a clean sacrifice which is our body, the temple of the Lord. Presenting our bodies as a living sacrifice means that we are not using our bodies as instruments of unrighteousness. In doing so, we take the temple of the Holy Spirit and present it to Satan for his unrighteous use.

A sacrifice is made when we are willing to give up something that is of great value and beneficial to us for the betterment of others or to gain something of greater significance. I have expressed on many occasions that the opposite of love is not hate. Hate is the absence of love. The opposite of love is selfishness. We present our bodies because it is pleasing to God and to show reverence, gratitude and worship for being allowed the privilege of housing the Holy Spirit (The returning of the Kingdom of God). If love is expressed through giving to benefit others then selfishness is the withholding of what you could give so that others will not benefit form what you could have shared. Sacrifice is another great expression of God's unconditional love abiding in us. When we are able to gain victory over and master this thing called selfishness we will then be able to walk as Christ walks in God's unconditional love toward others.

Sacrifice, an established Kingdom Law

Before the foundation of the world God established all of His Kingdom principles that would govern life in heaven as well as in the Earth. We see the Kingdom principle of sacrifice first introduced in the book of Genesis chapter 3 verses 21. The Word of God says, "Unto Adam also and unto his wife did the Lord God make coats of skins, and clothed them." After Adams sin we see his choice of clothing for he and Eve were fig leaves that they had sown together to hide their nakedness. However God's choice of clothing was the skins of an animal. Notice that in order for God to make coats of skins for them the principle of sacrifice had to be invoked. It simply says that something innocent must die so the guilty can go free. All throughout the Old Testament God required the children of Israel to offer a sacrifice for their sins. They were to kill an innocent animal of a certain age without blemish and have the blood poured on the mercy seat and then sprinkled on the people. This would serve as an acceptable sacrifice for the time until the true sacrifice should come. Even though the children of Israel were familiar with God's principle of sacrifice they were still blind to the true sacrifice which was the Lamb of God. When Jesus was brought before Pilate we see this great principle invoked. Just before the great demonstration of His love toward us we see the principle of sacrifice in its simplest form. The Jewish nation had a custom at the Passover that one condemned prisoner would be released. Pilate asked the question to the Jews saying, "Will you therefore that I release unto you the King of the Jews?" The angry crowd responded with, "Not this man, but Barabbas." Here we see the prelude to the ultimate sacrifice of love. A guilty robber and murderer were allowed a stay of execution because of the sacrifice of the King of Glory. He was not aware that in a few short hours the entire world from times past, present and future would be afforded the same stay of execution. Jesus the innocent died so mankind the guilty could go free.

The second portion of the sacrifice in the Old Testament only dealt with the covering or the moving forward of their sins and not the washing away of their sins. The scripture says, "And almost all things are by the law purged with blood; and without shedding of blood is no remission. Hebrews 9:22" This simply means that the cleansing agent that God used was the blood of animals. However the blood of animals had to be offered over and over again for each sin. The blood of animals had no power to take away sins. They could only be moved forward or covered. For the New Covenant to stand forever God had to use also an eternal sacrifice once and for all. He choose the sacrifice of His own Son and the shedding of His blood as the only acceptable sacrifice that was able to wash away the sins of mankind forever. "For if the blood of bulls and of goats, and the ashes of a heifer sprinkling the unclean, can sanctify to the purifying of the flesh: How much more shall the blood of Christ, who through the eternal Spirit offered himself without spot to God, purge (cleanse) your conscience from dead works to serve the living God? Hebrews 9:13-14" We are to be mindful that the principle of sacrifice has never changed only its application.

Sacrifice and commitment go hand in hand

I am a firm believer that you do not try God you commit to Him. Many are still trying God with little or no progress in life. Nothing of significance ever happens until there is a commitment. Commitment only takes place when my time, talent and treasures are available to God to accomplish His purpose with excellence, even if it means going above and beyond my initial expectation. I have found that these two, sacrifice and commitment, are two sides of the same coin. You cannot have one without the other. You will never make a commitment in an area you are not willing to sacrifice for and you will never sacrifice for something you are not committed to. God was so committed to His plan of salvation for the fallen world that He sacrificed His only begotten Son that whosoever believes on him will have everlasting life with Him. Jesus the King of Glory sacrificed himself on the cross at Calvary and shed His blood for you.

Sacrifice brings great reward

During a conversation that Jesus was having with the disciples Peter made the comment to the Lord that they had left all to follow Him. In response to Peter's statement the Lord responded with this, "Verily I say unto you, There is no man the has left house, or brothers, or sisters, or father, or mother, or wife, or children, or lands, for my sake, and the gospel's, but he shall receive a hundred fold now in this time, houses, and brothers, and sisters, and mothers, and children, and lands, with persecutions; and in the world to come eternal life." (St. Mark 10:29-30) Notice that in the previous scripture the sacrifices mentioned were all in the singular form. However, the repayment or rewards for the sacrifice made were all plural. One of the wonderful promises of God in His word is that He would multiply the seeds we sow.

Whenever I hear Christians speak evil of the men and women of God who preach the Word of God in sincerity and truth and are reaping the rewards of what the previous scripture promised I am saddened by the ignorance and the selfishness of those who should support the work of God and those that labor. God has promised in His Word that those who sacrifice their lives for Him will in no way lose out in this lifetime and shall be rewarded with eternal life as well. When you see the men and women of God enjoying the abundance that God has promised us in St John 10:10 we should rejoice with them. I want to take a moment and encourage those men and women of God who are benefiting from this promise. Don't be discouraged because of the persecution it is a part of the promised reward. Just know that if you are being persecuted for righteousness you are pleasing the Lord. Remember the hundredfold blessing comes with persecution. Hebrews 6:10 reminds us of this, "For God is not unrighteous to forget your work and labor of love, which you have showed toward his name, in that you have ministered to the saints and do minister." Stay encouraged your sacrifice is well pleasing to the Lord.

Evaluation

I have come to realize that in order to have more of God's presence I would have to make a greater sacrifice. I chose to sacrifice pleasing my flesh through unrighteousness so I could gain a greater understanding and appreciation of God's Holy Spirit. I sacrificed the comfort of my bed in the early morning so that I could honor God with the first of everyday through prayer and worship. I sacrificed the mindless entertainment of television for a deeper understanding of the principles of God through reading and studying His word. I have made many sacrifices that have paid untold dividends in my life. All of which I am so grateful to God and others for their encouragement and belief that God's will and purpose for my life would yield the harvest that He intended. Not that I have arrived or have no other sacrifices to make but that I am in a place of understanding through His grace. I want to take this moment to encourage you by stating, "Any success that you may have will always require a sacrifice." When He asks you to sacrifice something of value for the betterment of others trust Him and look forward to the rewards your sacrifice will bring. If you have not done so in prayer take the time and ask the Holy Spirit what sacrifices are required by God in order for you to obtain what God has for you. Therefore let us always be mindful of the Kingdom Principle of Sacrifice.

A Prayer for understanding

Heavenly Father, I come before you now realizing that you are requiring a sacrifice from me. Give me clarity and a desire to obey your instructions. Father I know that you have so much more in store for me and I am willing to make the necessary sacrifices to have the more of you. I know that sacrifice is also an attribute of love and I embrace that attribute right now for my benefit and the benefit of others so that you and you alone receive the glory and honor from the sacrifices that I make. Father, let me also recognize the importance and significance of the sacrifice Jesus made for me on the cross at Calvary. Thank you for your unchanging wisdom, knowledge, understanding and love. This I ask and receive by faith in the name of my Lord and Savior Jesus Christ. Amen.

Chapter 15

The Kingdom Principle of Sacrifice

Chapter Overview

Sacrifice- Romans 12:1 says, "I beseech you therefore bretheren, by the mercies of God, that you present your bodies a living sacrifice, holy, acceptable unto God, which is your reasonable service." God is still requiring a sacrifice form us today. Even though the application for sacrifice has changed the Kingdom Principle remains the same.

Sacrifice an Established Kingdom Law- Something innocent must die so the guilty can go free. God's demonstration in the Garden of Eden for Adam and Eve was just a shadow of things to come.

Sacrifice and commitment go hand in hand- They are two sides of the same coin. You will never make a sacrifice for something you are not committed to, and you will never fully commit in an area you are not willing to sacrifice for.

Sacrifice brings great reward- There is no sacrifice that we can make for Jesus and the gospel that we shall not be rewarded with an abundance of what we sacrificed and eternal life with Christ.

Evaluation- Ask the Holy Spirit to reveal to you the areas God is requiring you to make a sacrifice.

A Prayer for Understanding

CHAPTER 16

The Kingdom Principle of Offense

"A brother offended is harder to be won than a strong city; and their contentions are like the bars of a castle." Proverbs 18:19

"Then said he unto his disciples, It is impossible but that offenses will come: but woe unto him, through whom they come!" St. Luke 17:1

My mentor would often say, "The greatest sermon you can ever preach is the life you live before the people." When I first learned about the Kingdom Principle of Offense I was saddened by all of the times I had violated the principle. Not just for me but for those I had caused to stumble along the way. I have always had the kind of heart that never wants to see anyone hurt or suffer especially at my expense. It is the will of God that our lifestyle and walk before Him and others should mirror the life and walk of Jesus Christ. There are many things that can cause offense however one of the greatest is for the men and women of God to speak the truth of God's Word and then not live it before those to whom they have preached it to. I have said many times that a presentation without a demonstration is only conversation. In other words, both the words we preach (our presentation) and our actions (our demonstration) must mirror each other as the truth of God's Word.

Offense will always come

One of the great things about the Holy Spirit of God is that He has the ability to minister the Word of God with understanding to all those who hear it at the level of their comprehension. A ten year old will be able to understand the Word of God at their level just as a twenty-one year old will comprehend at his level. We are all at different levels of faith in our walk with God. Some are at a mature level of understanding and some are still maturing. Because of our different levels of spiritual maturity we are all subject to offense on some level. Those who are babes in Christ are easily offended because of their limited knowledge of God and His purpose. Whenever we don't have a clear understanding of something we are more susceptible to offense. We see this often when the commandment of tithing is taught. Those who are still maturing and ignorant of understanding are easily offended by the commands of God. Ignorance always enhances the offense. It is the desire of the enemy to keep you away from the truth of God's word so that this ignorance will reign and the assault through offense will continue to be enhanced.

All can relate

The biblical definition of offense is to cause one to fall into sinful ways. It is this definition that better explains the scripture in St.

Luke 17:1. Jesus said, "It is impossible but that offenses will come: but woe unto him, through whom they come." It is because of the fallen nature of man, his sinful ways and his participation in sinful activity that causes this type of offense. Whenever we participate in sin we become the servants to sin and we are doing the will of the one who is the master of sin. Sin leads us to a separation from God through our disobedience. Not only does it separate us but it causes us to experience the other definition of offense which is to hurt or cause pain. In the previous chapter entitled, "The Kingdom Principle of Forgiveness" I discussed that one of the reasons we face difficulties in life is because of human error. People can make mistakes, they can choose the wrong things and therefore cause themselves and others hurt and pain. This is an area that we can all relate to. Whenever we are faced with the situation of being offended because of someone else's actions we must remember what the Word of God has to say. Jesus said in St. Luke 17:2, "It were better for him that a millstone were hanged about his neck, an cast into the sea, than that he should offend one of these little ones." Jesus was telling them not to cause a child to participate in sin and cause them to fall into a sinful lifestyle. It is this sinful life style that will cause them to be hurt and feel the pains of life. In verse 3 Jesus gives us the antidote to this type of pain caused by others. He says, "Take heed to yourselves: if a brother trespasses (offend you) against thee, rebuke him; and if he repent, forgive him. The kingdom principle says that the way we stop the hurt and pain is to genuinely repent and forgive them.

Hurting people, hurt people

It has been said that relationships have been lost more by a few words than by a few actions. As children we would often say that, "Sticks and stones may break my bones but words will never hurt me." Wow! What a statement. As we know our words have the power of life and death. There is nothing sweeter than encouraging and uplifting words of approval and there is nothing more devastating than words that cause us pain. One of the key components of the kingdom principle of sowing and reaping is that a seed reproduces after its own kind. A seed is any word you say, action you do or thought you think. Since our words are seeds and they proceed out of our heart, we can always determine the condition of our heart by the words we speak. Jesus said in Matthew 12:34b, "... for out of the abundance of the heart the mouth speaks." Verse 35-37, "A good man out of the good treasures of the heart brings forth good things: and an evil man out of the evil treasure brings forth evil things. But I say unto you, that every idle word that men shall speak, they shall give account thereof in the Day of Judgment. For by thy words thou shall be justified, and by thy words thou shall be condemned." People who have been hurt have hidden away in their heart the hurt they feel. When something or someone reminds them of the offense that caused the hurt they begin to reveal that hurt through their words and eventually their actions. Those who speak words that offend and hurt are also hurt themselves. You can always tell a wounded spirit by the words that proceed from their mouth. Evil and hurtful words indicate an evil and hurtful heart. An evil heart is always the result of a previous hurt that has not been healed by the blood of Jesus. One thing to remember is that offense is causing a person hurt or pain or to cause someone to fall into sinful ways. Whenever we choose not to forgive or to genuinely repent we are in error and in essence we are saying that I don't believe the blood of Jesus has the power to heal this hurt. In doing so, we forsake the King and the principle that can cause the pain to be healed.

Words of warning

Using the principle of the power of four we can understand that there are four distinct actions through words that will warn us of other persons hurts. Whenever words are spoken that demonstrate one, all or a combination of the following you can be confident that the person speaking has not been healed from a previous offense. I call them the (4) C's of offense. Those words are demonstrated through the following:

1. Cursing- These are words of profanity. They are usually meant to defame, demoralize and destroy another.
2. Criticizing- to find unmerited fault in another. To demean or speak evil of in an offensive manner.
3. Condemning- pronouncing unfair or unwarranted judgment, or strong disapproval through words or actions.
4. Complaining- to express feeling of pain, dissatisfaction and annoyance.

Whenever you hear these types of commentary coming from the mouths of others they are the warning signs that an offense has occurred and has not been properly dealt with using the kingdom principles of the Word of God. I have come to view it as their way of communicating that they are looking for someone who can help them get their heart healed. What an awesome opportunity for ministry. Instead of being offended by what they are saying view it as a warning sign to get involved and an opportunity to share with them the good news of Jesus Christ. If the offense is directed at you it is their way of saying I believe you are the one who can help me. It took me awhile to understand it, but the Lord shared with me that if I would be willing to look past the words and the direct attack I would be able to see their hurt and direct them to His healing power of forgiveness and redemption.

Healing the offended

"Bretheren, if any man be overtaken in a fault, you which are spiritual, restore such a one in the spirit of meekness; considering yourself, lest you also be tempted. Bear you one another's burden and so fulfill the law of Christ." Galatians 6:1-2

It is not God's intentions that His children live this present life in the bondage of past hurts and offenses. Jesus paid the ultimate price so that we could be healed form all of our past hurts. All that He endured on the cross that day was for our benefit. He gave us another chance to come back into right standing with the Father and Himself. With the help of the Holy Spirit we no longer have to live a life of hurt and pain. Thank you Lord!!!

The Lord's mission as it is outlined in Isaiah 61:1-3 tells of His great love for us and His desire that we be made whole. It says, "The Spirit of the Lord God is upon me; because the Lord has anointed me to preach good tidings unto the meek; he has sent me to bind up the broken hearted, to proclaim liberty to the captives, and the opening of the prison to them that are bound; to proclaim the acceptable year of the Lord, and the day of vengeance of our God; to comfort all that mourn; To appoint unto them that mourn in Zion, to give unto them beauty for ashes, the oil of joy for mourning, the garment of praise for the spirit of heaviness; that they might be called trees of righteousness, the planting of the Lord that He might be glorified." He is ready at this very moment to heal you. Will you let Him?

A prayer for healing

Heavenly Father, in the name of Jesus I come to you now with a heart that needs your healing touch. You said in your Word that Jesus came to bind up the broken hearted. Father my heart has been hurt. I ask that you heal my broken heart now with your love. Cover me with the blood of Jesus. Father, I forgive those who have caused me to be offended and hurt. I ask that you forgive me for the offenses and hurts I have caused others. Father set me free right now so that I am no longer held in bondage by my past feelings. I surrender all of my past hurts to you. Thank you, Father, for your mercy and forgiveness and for healing my broken heart. In Jesus name I pray Amen.

Chapter 16

The Kingdom Principle of Offense

Overview

It is the will of God, that our lifestyle and walk before Him and others should mirror the life and walk of Christ.

Offenses will always come- It is the desire of the enemy to keep you away from the truth of God's word so that this ignorance will reign and the assault through offense will continue to be enhanced.

All can relate- The biblical definition of offense is to cause someone to fall into sinful ways.

Hurting people, hurt people- An evil heart is always the result of a previous hurt that has not been healed by the blood of Jesus.

Words of warning- Whenever words of cursing, criticizing, condemnation and complaining are spoken you can be confident that the persons heart has not been healed.

Healing the offense- It is not God's will that His children live this present life in the bondage of past hurts and offenses.

A Prayer for healing

CHAPTER 17

The Kingdom Principle of Prosperity/Financial Freedom

"If therefore you have not been faithful in the unrighteous mammon, who will commit to your trust the true riches? And if you have not been faithful in that which is another man's, who shall give you that which is your own?" St. Luke 16:12-13

"For I know the thoughts that I think toward you, says the Lord, thoughts of peace, and not of evil, to give you an expected end." Jeremiah 29:11

As I sat in the sanctuary and listened to my mentor speak he began to talk about prosperity. He approached the subject with great conviction as he does all of his messages but this day there was a very noticeable anointing that was present. It was the kind of anointing for revelation. As he spoke the scripture came to mind in 2 Timothy 3:16. It states, "All scripture is given by inspiration of God, and is profitable for doctrine, for reproof, for correction, for instruction in righteousness." The specific part of the scripture that was standing out was the part that says it is good for reproof. The word reproof in this passage means the dismantling or the tearing down of erroneous thinking. As he continued to speak he went on to say, "One of the most difficult things to do is to get someone to change an erroneous belief that was established in church." For years there has been a debate about the financial abundance that is being displayed by the prominent men and women of God. My position is not to debate your opinion about what should or should not be but to encourage the believer to seek out the Kingdom principle that allows you to best be positioned to fulfill God purpose and plan for your life. In order to do that you must embrace the truth about the Kingdom principle of prosperity and financial freedom.

A lack of knowledge

The prophet Hosea states in chapter 4 verses 6a, "My people are destroyed for lack of knowledge..." Knowledge is spiritual truth and the only truth is the Word of God. Jesus said in St. John 17:17, "Sanctify them through thy truth: thy word is truth." In order to tear down erroneous thinking, the word of God must be applied. Such is the case when we hear error about the kingdom principle of prosperity and financial freedom. It is not the will of God that His children remain in bondage in any area of life this also includes the area of finances. However we know that there are many who have accepted Christ and have been redeemed by his sacrifice on the cross that are still living in bondage even though the price for their sins and iniquities has been paid in full. They are being destroyed and are still living in bondage because they refuse to, or may not know how to apply the truth (the Word of God) to those areas of life. Jesus said in St. John 8:32, "And you shall know the truth, and the truth shall make you free." Here the Lord states that it is only the truth you know that will make you free. The Holy Spirit reminded me once that the only thing you know is what you actually apply. You may know of it but the truth of knowing is only found when that knowledge is applied. So in other words; you can apply the knowledge (the spiritual truth) to the situation and that application of truth is what will make you free. The principle of faith relies on spiritual truth so much that the Word of God teaches us that we are to add to our faith virtue; and to virtue knowledge (2 Peter 1:5). Having faith in God depends on the spiritual knowledge you have. In order to increase your faith you have to also increase in the spiritual knowledge you have of Christ. The word in 2 Peter 3:18 says, "But grow in grace, and in the knowledge of our Lord and Savior Jesus Christ…"

Prosperity, what is it exactly?

During my search for the definition of prosperity I came a cross several meanings from a few different sources. Each of the sources used a common key word. That word was successful. Successful means to accomplish based upon given expectations. Even when we think of prosperity as having all sufficiency in resources we can also apply the definition of having accomplished a task based upon expectations. From a spiritual point of view prosperity begins and ends with God's purpose. We can easily determine if we are living by the Kingdom principle of Prosperity because we will be living based on God's purpose for our life. One of the other phrases that were a constant in the definitions was the phrase financial abundance. Abundance means having sufficiency or more than enough. Prosperity then can be described as accomplishing God's expectation which is your purpose and having all sufficiency, or having more than enough resources to accomplish it. This definition of prosperity must encompass all (7) areas of your life. My mentor often says, "That God will never call you to a set of objectives and then with hold the resources you need to get the job done." Purpose already has provisions accounted for.

Established by God

In an earlier chapter I mention a quote from Bishop I.V. Hilliard he stated, "That whenever God establishes something in human history he establishes its priority." Soon after during my study and prayer time the Holy Spirit began to minister to me this truth. He not only presented this statement as truth but He also expounded on it for me. Shortly after, He gave me a complete and greater understanding of it. The Holy Spirit said that there were (7) total things that God establishes whenever any thing is established in human history. He revealed to me that (6) of the established things are performed by God and that He requires man to establish the seventh one. He stated that this is where true prosperity is obtained. He said, "Whenever God establishes something in human history He establishes the following (6) things." They are:

1. Its purpose – The reason for the existence of a thing.
2. Its priority – The order of its importance.
3. Its provisions – The substance necessary to sustain it.

4. Its position – Who you will learn from and who you will teach.
5. Its potential- What it is capable of or what is possible.
6. Its place – Where it will have jurisdiction and authority.

Go back and look at each one of these things that God establishes and plug into it your own life and ministry. These are vital pieces of information to know. They are critical to your living out the Kingdom principle of prosperity and financial freedom.

The seventh thing that is established is equally as important for you to understand. As the Holy Spirit spoke I began to reflect on the awesome love and grace that our Lord has provided us. I began to think about why the Lord disapproves of excuses. Through the finished works of Christ we have been given the opportunity to be brought back into a right relationship with the Father, regain the Kingdom and therefore are entitled to all that Christ has merited for us on the cross. This includes Gods original plan for man to reign with his Son as kings in the earth. However we were created as free willed moral agents with the ability to receive or reject Christ. With this information I clearly understood why He has left it up to us to establish the seventh one. Just remember the number seven in the Kingdom of God is a number that represents completion. The seventh one that has to be established by you and you alone is:

7. Its performance- What it will do and how it will behave.

Once you have established what performance you will give God the process of living out the Kingdom principle of prosperity and financial freedom has begun.

Financial principles in the Word of God to live by

"Trust in the Lord with all thine heart; and lean not to your own understanding. In all your ways acknowledge him and he shall direct thy path." Proverbs 3:5-6

"Honor the Lord with thy substance, and with the first fruits of all thy increase: So shall thy barns be filled with plenty, and thy presses shall burst out with new wine." Proverbs 3:9-10

"And thou say in thine heart, my power and the might of my hand hath gotten me this wealth. But thou shall remember the Lord thy God: for it is he that gives thee power to get wealth that he may establish his covenant which he swear unto thy fathers, as it is this day." Deuteronomy 8:17-18

"Bring ye all the tithes into the store house, that there may be meat in my house, and prove me now says the Lord of hosts, if I will not open you the windows of heaven, and pour you out a blessing, that there shall not be room enough to receive it. And I will rebuke the devourer for your sakes, and he shall not destroy the fruits of your ground; neither shall your vine cast her fruit before the time in the field, says the Lord of hosts. And all nations shall call you blesses: for you shall be a delightsome land, says the Lord of hosts." Malachi 3:10-12

"Give and it shall be given unto you; good measure, pressed down, and shaken together, and running over, shall men give into your bosom. For with the same measure that you mete with all it shall be measured to you again." St. Luke 6:38

"The thief comes not, but for to steal, and to kill, and to destroy: I am come that they might have life, and that they might have it more abundantly." St. John 10:10

"But this I say, He whom sows sparingly shall reap also sparingly; and he which sows bountifully shall reap also bountifully. Every man according as he purposes in his heart, so let him give; not grudgingly, or of necessity: for God loves a cheerful giver. And God is able to make all grace abound toward you; that you always having all sufficiency in all things, may abound to every good work; (As it is written, He has dispersed abroad; he has given to the poor: his righteousness remains forever. Now he that ministers seed to the sower both minister bread for your food, and multiply your seed sown, and increase the fruits of your righteousness;) 2 Corinthians 9:6-10

"Let him that is taught in the word communicate unto him that teaches in all good things. Be not deceived; God is not mocked: for whatsoever a man sows that shall he also reap. For he that sows to his flesh shall of the flesh reap corruption; but he that sows to the Spirit shall of the Spirit reap life everlasting. And let us not be weary in well doing: for in due season we shall reap, if we faint not. As we have therefore opportunity, let us do good unto all men, especially unto them of the household of faith." Galatians 6:6-10

"Knowing that whatsoever good any man does, the same shall he receive of the Lord, whether he is bond or free." Ephesians 6:8

"It is God which works in you both to will and to do his good pleasure." Philippians 2:13

"That you might walk worthy of the Lord unto all pleasing, being fruitful in every good work, and increasing in the knowledge of God." Colossians 1:10

"Charge them that are rich in the world, that they be not high minded, nor trust in uncertain riches, but in the living God, who gives us richly all things to enjoy. That they do good, that they be rich in good works, ready to distribute, willing to communicate; Laying up in store for themselves a good foundation against the time to come, that they may lay hold on eternal life." 1Timothy 6:17-19

A Final thought

The prosperity principle is a kingdom principle that applies to all of God's children. It covers the totality of all of your life. It can only be measured by the completion of God's purpose. Included in the purpose are the financial provisions necessary to accomplish the purpose. Just like any of God's principles it must also be taught in truth. To exclude the other areas of life and only focus on the financial side of prosperity is teaching the principle incorrectly and it creates a false balance. The principle has to be taught in conjunction with purpose. The previous scriptures all give us an insight as to how God measure true prosperity. Take time daily to study them and commit them to your heart. They will help you in understanding why God wants you to be prosperous and what you are to do with the provisions that accompany your purpose.

My mentor would often remind me, that you must be a principled driven individual in order to live out God's purpose and plan and to enjoy the totality of your prosperity. It is all for the glory of God, your benefit and the benefit of others.

Take time to study the Kingdom principles that are written in this book and apply them. The application of any one of God's principles will bring tangible increase into your life.

A Prayer for you

Heavenly Father,

My prayer to you is for the children of God, that you will grant them the wisdom, knowledge and understanding necessary to fulfill the purpose that you have created them for, and that they continue to grow in the knowledge of our Lord and savior Jesus Christ and that they be lead by the Holy Spirit of promise. Bless the doers of the principles of the word of God and cause the tangible increase to be multiplied in their lives. In the name of Jesus Christ our King I pray.

The grace of our Lord and Savior Jesus Christ is with your spirit. Amen.

Chapter 17

The Kingdom Principle of Prosperity/ Financial Freedom

Overview

Reproof- The dismantling or the tearing down of erroneous thinking

A Lack of knowledge- People are destroyed because of their lack of Spiritual truth (The Word of God)

Prosperity, what is it really? - The prosperity message has to encompass the totality of life and not just financial abundance. To teach it any other way is to teach in error and to cause an imbalance.

Established by God- Whenever God establishes something in human history He establishes these (7) things, six are done by Him, the seventh must be established by you.

Financial Principles in the Word of God to live by- These (12) scriptures will give you a great understanding of the financial promises God makes to the believer.

A Final Thought- The prosperity principle covers all of God's children and it is His will that you live out the purpose in which you were created. Living out purpose reveals your provisions.

A Prayer for you

CPSIA information can be obtained
at www.ICGtesting.com
Printed in the USA
LVOW12s1321301117
558149LV00001B/100/P